LIVE HAPPILY
WITH THE WOMAN
YOU LOVE

LIVE HAPPILY
WITH THE WOMAN
YOU LOVE

By
GODFREY W. EXEL

MOODY PRESS
CHICAGO

© 1977 by
THE MOODY BIBLE INSTITUTE
OF CHICAGO

Library of Congress Cataloging in Publication Data

Exel, Godfrey W.
  Live happily with the woman you love.
  1. Marriage. 2. Husbands. I. Title.

BV835.E94   248'.842   77-10744

ISBN 0-8024-4900-X

Printed in the United States of America

To my wife, Betty, whose faith, working through love, has often led me when I should have been leading her. To Bob, Ann, Jerry, and Arlene, our children, who often are used to teach me when I should be teaching them.

Live happily with the woman you love through the fleeting days of life, for the wife God gives you is your best reward down here for all your earthly toil (Ecclesiastes 9:9, *The Living Bible*).

Contents

Introduction

One can easily see that the world is ruled by a power structure and that wealth is an important ingredient in attaining and wielding power. There is a satanic conspiracy grappling for the minds of men everywhere. Blindness leads men to believe that good can accomplish nothing of permanence and that evil is in the ascendancy. In the struggle for self-survival, man is a victim of the world system.

The idealism of youth cannot long survive this system of competition, power, and wealth; a system, in the words of C. I. Scofield, "often outwardly religious, scientific, cultured, and elegant; but, seething with national and commercial rivalries and ambitions, [it] is upheld in any real crisis only by armed force, and is dominated by Satanic principles."[1]

My own struggle to remain idealistic ceased during the difficult World War II years, when I served in the U.S. Navy. As far as the world system was concerned, I decided: If you can't lick 'em, join 'em. I was going to achieve recognition in this mad, mad world through money and power. On my return to civilian life, I set out to do it.

Postwar marriage and children soon revealed that I was not only a bitter cynic about life, but also a driving, self-centered man bent on worldly achievement and success, incapable of real love. Oh, I knew about the kind of love that makes Hollywood and the world go around, and I used the word *love* very casually. It is easy to call gratification of our needs "love." But I knew nothing about the love of God that provides a foundation for building a life and a home, and that reaches out to others with a helping hand. I was hurting too much to help anyone. In his book *Why Am I Afraid to Love?*, John Powell says, "I once asked a psychiatrist friend of mine, 'How can you teach people to love?' His answer was mildly surprising, to say the least. He answered the question by asking one of his own: 'Did you ever have a toothache? Of whom were you thinking during the distress of your toothache?' His point was clear. When we are in pain, even if it be only the passing discomforts of an aching tooth, we are thinking about ourselves."[2]

The pain-filled world I grew up in is the same one we all occupy. The pain is much greater than a mere toothache, for which there are simple remedies. God reaches us with

His love through human beings. Through the love of my wife and children, He reached me. Through their growing and continuing love and that of other people, I continue to experience His eternal love and healing power.

I was thirty-seven when I became a Christian and began building on the foundation of God's love and His Word. When I began to write this book, I wanted to dedicate it to the Book of books, the Bible. Its pages have revealed more and more of His love for me. But I thought this might seem theological and stuffy. So the human instruments of His love, my family, became the object of my dedication.

I want to achieve a twofold objective: to help men presently out of touch with their wives, win them to themselves, and, if need be, to Christ; and then, to impress men with their responsibility to assume loving leadership in their homes.

There is a way of life that helps heal the hurts and turns us from ourselves to others. This way of life is predicated on the selfless love of God—a love we can appropriate and practice. It is a love born of faith, quite apart from human love and its dependence on human emotions. This godly love teaches us how to deny self, die to self, and take up the work of winning others. He has given us this task of communicating His love to others, and it is an awesome responsibility. It begins at home, and it should start with the husband.

For many years my wife, Betty, and I were involved with Campus Crusade for Christ, International. Although it is principally a ministry of young men and women reaching out to the college and university campuses with the Good News of Christ, we became a part of the lay division in its early days. The thrust of the lay ministry was teaching men, women, and young people how to share the reality of Christ with others and how to live more fruitful and happy lives.

To assist us in our teaching and counseling roles, Dr. Henry Brandt, then Campus Crusade for Christ staff psychologist, taught us much about personal counseling. In our summer staff training sessions, the senior staff spent much time in this type of preparation. As a result of our training and a lifetime of experience in raising our own family, my wife and I have been used to help many in their marriage difficulties and child-rearing responsibilities.

Recently I suffered an accident that inactivated me for several months. The lack of physical activity led me to my typewriter to work over some manuscripts written while we were establishing the Campus Crusade for Christ lay ministry in New Zealand.

During this time of inactivity, I immersed myself in books on the "how to" of having a successful marriage and a happy home life. What appalled me was that most of these books currently in vogue are written to women and seem to place the main responsibility for a successful home squarely on the shoulders of the wife. This is not God's plan at all! The responsibility rests on the man.

So I want to tell it where it counts. Wives, are you reading this so you will know where the real responsibility for a happy home lies? Husbands, are you reading and paying attention as I unburden myself to you? You are the one whom God has chosen to bear the leadership of the family. If you are willing to investigate this, read on, and let us save our wives from the self-destructive course of taking all the blame for a poor marriage.

1

There Has to Be Something More

"Honey, I'm going to spend the rest of my life making love to you, night and day." The words of a song? Yes, but more importantly, they are the words I used in pledging my love to Betty just before we were married.

Equally well chosen for the occasion were her words, "Oh, darling, I love you, and I'm going to spend the rest of my life making you the happiest man in the world!" This was a good way to begin a lifelong commitment, don't you think?

Someone has said it is easy to write the first chapter of a book. Yes, and it is just as easy to begin a marriage on sweet sentiments and empty words. The early joys of marriage that come with having a wife are very sweet, indeed. Why does marriage have to become less and less joy and more and more indifference as time goes on?

Children come along, not always as planned, even in this day of enlightenment. The responsibilities mount, and the nitty-gritty of daily life begins to get to us, disillusioning and leading us to wonder about the purpose of it all. Our ambitions and desires are frustrated; our goals always seem just beyond our grasp.

Our human appetites are never satisfied. Samuel Gompers, the English labor organizer who accomplished so much in American unionism, was once asked, "Just what do your men want in your union?"

His thoughtful reply was, "More!"

John D. Rockefeller was once asked, "Just how much money does a man have to have, anyway?"

His answer was, "Just a little bit more."

Solomon, the wisest of Israel's kings, had a thousand wives and concubines. Still he wanted more, more, more. Nothing seems to satisfy the fires of our longings completely. There is always an inner restlessness. Are we naive enough to think any woman can satisfy us for a lifetime? Do we think just because we have a wife, home, and many other things we long for that we are going to be satisfied and live happily ever after?

No matter what the course of our lives, no matter what successes are achieved, we find that we are still empty men, experiencing what Jean Paul Sartre calls "existential loneliness." Our ego conflicts, and sometimes strong, aggressive desires are devastating to our peace of mind and threaten our marriages and homes. Perhaps the sexual relationship we have with our wives never becomes what we dreamed it would. Our strong, self-centered egos immediately blame our partner, raising communication barriers between husband and wife.

In the beginning God ordained marriage to provide mutual aid, fellowship and perpetuation of the species. To make man complete, God performed a rib-removing operation on Adam and made a woman for him. The word *woman* literally means "because she was taken out of man." This relationship was to be so close that husbands and wives were to become "one flesh," as typified in the sexual union. God meant this union to be the most exciting experience of our lives. God liked what He made because we were in His image. His desire for us was to have fellowship with Him and be fruitful and multiply in order to populate the earth and control it (Genesis 2:18-23).

Things were good for Adam! God provided for every need and then some. There was no competition for Eve. Perhaps she asked her husband, "Adam, do you love me?" His reply would have to be, "Of course, Eve. Who else?"

Adam and Eve had no money problems, no politics, no taxes. However, trouble was on the way. Soon Eve listened to the serpent in the garden, and ignoring the command of God, she persuaded Adam to cooperate with her in disobeying God. This resulted in God's driving them out of the garden because of their disobedience.

The Great Cop-out

You remember how Adam passed the buck and said to God, "the woman whom *Thou* gavest to be with me" caused me to disobey and eat the forbidden fruit (Genesis 3:12, italics added). "The woman *you* gave me, God. You are to blame for all my problems. So why shouldn't I go my own way and do my own thing?" And we have been running from Him ever since those days in the Garden of Eden.

Since that day in the garden, our cop-out has been to blame our wives, our mothers or someone else. Some of our not-so-manly blame-placing expressions go like this: "I have to work like this because my wife wants so many things." Or, "I am an adulterer because of my frigid wife." Or, "I spend so much time with the boys because my wife is such a nag." Or, "My mother (or mother-in-law) is my problem."

Marriage on the Run

Marriage is now in such disfavor that fewer and fewer want to be in it for keeps. "Get in, and get out of it doesn't work" is the current philosophy. Maybe you have been in it for a few difficult, tiring years and the "urge to merge" has become a "force for divorce." But if you are experiencing the kind of marriage God ordained for you, your oneness with your wife will be indivisible. It will go much deeper than that typified by the sexual union. Your relationship will be enriched more and more as your devotion to Christ grows.

Other Gods Take Over

As a young man, I used to spend much time lying awake at night trying to figure out what had gone wrong with my marriage. I knew instinctively that something was missing.

There had to be more to life than I was experiencing, something more than a good wife, lovely children, and a business that was providing an abundance of material things.

At this point in life, I experienced subtle changes in behavior. The excitement of business began to overshadow the desire to have a happy home. I was meeting more and more often with my business associates for breakfast, lunch and dinner. We were planning greater business expansion and outreach. I plunged into my favorite escapes. Football games and other athletic pursuits took more of my free evenings and weekends. I ardently pursued fishing and hunting. I found myself avoiding my family. The strange gods of a man's world helped fill the vacuum in my life. They created an increasingly greater barrier between my family and me.

I would not tell you this personal experience if it were not so typical of husband-wife relationships today. Men use numerous avoidance patterns to escape their responsibilities to their wives and families. Our inadequacies and ineptitudes drive us first one way and then another in our search for a way out.

Strange Ways of Escape

Much is written about neurotic women, but the battle of life leaves the wreckage of neurotic men everywhere. The human flotsam found in the skid rows of any city are testimony to the result of men at war with themselves. Carl C. Jung, in *Modern Man in Search of a Soul,* defines neurosis as "an inner cleavage—the state of being at war with oneself."[1] It is a neurotic world, all right. The inner wars of men are expressed outwardly in those of civilization.

A typical example is a couple I know. There is little or no communication between them. The wife is lonely, misunderstood, frustrated, and fearful. When there is something unpleasant or stressful to face, the husband escapes into avoidance patterns. He becomes uncommunicative, tense, resorting to alcoholic beverages and staring at television for hours on end. Frequently he gets into his car and without explanation goes away for extended periods of time.

His actions have only brought on guilt feelings, shame at the way he mistreats his wife (he sometimes becomes physically abusive) and fear of being found out for what he really is. Outwardly he appears to be a successful businessman with a beautiful wife, lovely home, and big car, as well as some expensive toys, such as an airplane and a boat. Inwardly, he is in a state of morbid dejection and sadness at the mess he has made of his personal life. At times he becomes so discouraged and depressed that he arrives at a state of utter despair. This is often the road to alcoholism, or even suicide.

Sometimes the reality of life as a father and husband, with its heavy responsibilities, is more than we can bear. When we are unable to cope, we often hide behind anger and antisocial behavior. Our failure to be the kind of husbands and fathers we want to be may lead to actual physical sickness. One fine, young, family man who worked several years for me used to lose contact with reality to such an extent that he would turn himself into our state hospital for the mentally ill. There he could make up his own kind of world without any responsibility. When he tired of his escape, a "cure" would result, and he could face life, wife and children again until the next family crisis came.

Of all the routes we take to escape our God-given responsibilities as fathers and husbands, the route of addiction is the saddest. Once a compulsive attachment to alcohol or drugs begins to rule us, we usually prefer our addiction to anything or anyone else. Even work, play, fantasy, food, or intellectual and religious "trips" can become addictions of a kind. More demands more when such addiction begins, and the situation usually worsens with each passing year. Once a certain point is passed, the man (or woman) in a state of addiction may be so helpless he can live only in the condition he has chosen for himself, unwilling to change, not able to see any alternatives to his present plight.

These addictions stem from an emptiness that seems impossible to fill. The feast of the honeymoon will not satisfy us. The wisdom and ever-learning of a Solomon will not satisfy us. The riches Solomon sought and attained, his vast public works and home construction programs will not satisfy us. Is there no peace, no rest? There has to be something more!

2

Who Does the Dishes?

I grew up with the notion that men were made of Spartan stuff. Courage, fortitude, and discipline prevented a show of emotion. Tears were the exclusive realm of the female. Furthermore, daily tasks were divided into men's work and women's work, and never the twain should meet! For a man to do dishes was tantamount to weeping in public. To venture into the female world was traitorous for the male, and if you were caught doing it, you were marked as one of them. Even cosmetics belonged exclusively to the female world. But the revolution of the sixties did away with most of these notions, and the women's lib movement of the seventies should remove vestigial traces.

Who does what around the house is no part of the courtship, marriage or honeymoon package. Those sensible enough to seek premarital counseling by a qualified pastor or marriage counselor may not find household duties a part of the general course. Barring illness or children, the question may never become a problem.

When I was courting Betty, I so dearly loved to be with her every moment, I even had the courage to forsake my male role long enough to help her with the dishes when she invited me to her parents' home for meals. It is funny how quickly I reverted to my traditional position after the wedding march!

How long can a man keep from helping a worn-out, harried mother of four children? There is no way to deny that the female is not as strong physically as the male. In that sense, at least, she is the weaker sex. The fact that we are so reluctant to help a mother and wife who is obviously overworked just proves how our old, self-centered natures are oblivious to the needs of those closest to us.

Sometimes the Christian husband and father is as achievement oriented and position aspiring as those without Christ. And that is when trouble starts, even in a Christian marriage.

I remember the early years of our marriage. Not only did I work six and sometimes seven days a week in my crazy pursuit of promotion, higher salary and success, but I usually worked two or three nights. When the weekend arrived, no one dared stand in the way of my relaxation and rest, which usually turned out to be a fishing or hunting trip lasting until the wee hours of the morning. Exhausted from my "rest and relaxation," I generally was so crabby that the family could not stand me until I had a day or two of rest back at work! So how could I have time and energy to help my wife with the kids and with boring chores around the house?

Paul wrote to Timothy, "But realize this, that in the last days difficult times will come. For men will be lovers of self, lovers of money, boastful, arrogant, revilers, disobedient to parents, ungrateful, unholy, unloving, irreconcilable, malicious gossips, without self-control, brutal, haters of good, treacherous, reckless, conceited, lovers of pleasure rather than lovers of God" (2 Timothy 3:1-4).

A Committed Wife

When my eldest son was twelve, my wife was struggling to hold the family together and to establish a foundation on which the children could build meaningful lives. She had been to a series of meetings conducted by a young evangelist. One day his sermon was taken from a text in the Old Testament. He went back some thirty-five hundred years, describing the Israelites, free of their slavery to the Egyptians and wandering in the Sinai Desert. They were continually longing for the things they had enjoyed in Egypt. They were constantly serving false gods—gods of licentious living, of the belly, of sexual immorality, of unrestraint, and of pleasure.

While they were being led out of slavery into the land God had promised, their wanderings took them through harsh, mountainous wastes and barren deserts. The temptation to go back into their old ways and indulge their insatiable appetite in pleasure was at times overpowering. Their proneness to worship false gods also showed up continually, even though they had seen convincing demonstrations of Jehovah's power.

Joshua was old and weary. Just before his death, he gave this last charge to the Israelites: "Now, therefore, fear the LORD and serve Him in sincerity and truth; and put away the gods which your fathers served beyond the River and in Egypt, and serve the LORD. And if it is disagreeable in your sight to serve the LORD, choose for yourselves today whom you will serve . . . but as for me and my house, we will serve the Lord" (Joshua 24:14-15).

That day my wife came home with her choice made. As for her and her house, they were going to serve the Lord. At that moment, her life began to change remarkably. I had failed to take my proper place of leadership under God in the family, so she was going to do something about it!

Recalling those days when my wife, overworked and frail, was willing to make further sacrifices to teach our children the principles for a good life embarrasses me now. I was so determined to have my own way that I used to arise very early on Sunday and spend the entire day fishing, hunting, or in other selfish pursuits. Meanwhile, she struggled with four growing children, readying them for Sunday school and church so they could have Christian instruction.

FATHERS, TEACH YOUR CHILDREN

In another Old Testament passage, God's appointed leader, Moses, told the Israelites that God had made a contract with them at Mount Horeb. "The LORD did *not make this covenant with our fathers, but with us, with all those of us alive here today"* (Deuteronomy 5:3, italics added.) Then Moses reviewed the laws given to them by God and explained the purpose for them: "So that you and your son and your grandson might fear the Lord your God, to keep all His statutes and His commandments, which I command you, all the days of your life, and that your days may be prolonged" (Deuteronomy 6:2). The exhortation that follows is important to husbands and fathers: "And these words, which I am commanding you today, shall be on your heart; and you shall teach them diligently to your sons and shall talk of them when you sit in your house and when you walk by the way and when you lie down and when you rise up" (Deuteronomy 6:6-7). Of course, your wife should assist in teaching them, under your leadership and direction, as God intended. But the responsibility is ours as fathers.

One Sunday morning my wife was struggling to feed the children, do the dishes, dress our little gals and guys, and get them off to church. I was using alternate plan number two for Sundays. Instead of seeking refuge in the great outdoors (where I vowed my worship was just as meaningful as hers), I was sleeping in, resting my poor, overworked self. As usual, my sleep was a pretense to avoid being part of the "as for me and my house, we will serve the Lord" routine. I was waiting for them to leave so I could arise in peace and serve myself breakfast, then bury my head in the Sunday paper until time for the family to come home for dinner.

Just before Betty and the children left for church, my pillowed head heard my eldest son say, "Aw gee, Mom, why do I have to go to Sunday school and church. Dad never goes." *Poor boy,* I tried to think, *His Mom sure is pushy on this Sunday school and church routine.* Nevertheless, I was ashamed of my conduct. Her good example only emphasized my negligence.

The next Sunday, making a martyr of myself, I made my first stab at leading my family to church. Compelled by shame, but inwardly unwilling and rebellious, I arose a trifle later than I should have, making the family late for church. Then I proceeded to sleep through most of the preacher's sermon. Never wanting to go again, I made

24

Betty's life miserable on the way home and for the rest of the day. If she had left me then, my fate would have been deserved. When husbands display attitudes like mine was, it is no wonder that wives soon forget the excitement of romance and the undying vows of yesterday. A root of bitterness takes their place.

Faith Comes from Hearing

Where did our family go from there? Shame and guilt were already doing their work in my conscience. In addition, God, using my wife and our kitchen radio, brought me to my senses.

One thing I greatly admire about my wife is that she rises early and prepares a nourishing breakfast for me and the children. While preparing breakfast, wanting to grow in spiritual wisdom and knowledge, she listens to a Christian radio station. It just happened that when I arrived at the table for breakfast, a well-known Bible teacher from the Midwest was beginning his daily Bible lesson. I wanted nothing to do with her "as for me and my house we will serve the Lord" philosophy. Nor did I want to listen to her daily radio lessons. Mornings were enough of a hassle without having to put up with that!

One morning my irritation surfaced. I barked, "Shut that radio off!" Looking hurt, but without saying a word, she obliged. In a depressed mood, I left for the office, realizing that too many mornings were this way. However, I seemed powerless to change them.

The next morning, to my surprise, she had the radio on very softly. I felt like throwing it out the window, but my shame from the previous morning restrained me. I tried not to listen. Each morning thereafter it was on—each day a little louder. I thought I would try to be a forebearing husband and exercise patience by putting up with it. But my disposition only seemed to worsen with the passing weeks.

At this stage in our marriage, I had borrowed money and mortgaged everything we had, to go into business with a lifelong friend of mine. He had been my boss for a few years prior to our business venture. Our business was "my baby," so to speak. I had conceived it and persuaded my old friend and boss to give up his executive position and chance it with me in electrical wholesale distribution. We were beginning to taste the fruits of mild success. Nothing else mattered. Business was my number-one priority. Everyone could see the huge dollar signs in my eyeballs!

The radio preacher droned on every morning, and "faith comes from hearing, and hearing by the word of Christ" (Romans 10:17). After two years of it, I caught myself humming some of the religious songs sung by his quartet and vocal ensemble. As the pressures of business and home increased, so did my sense of frustration. Success and material gain did not accomplish what, in earlier years, I had thought would be the sure result. New cars, new toys for men, and more expensive vacations only seemed to add to my sense of aimlessness and uselessness.

A COMMITTED HUSBAND

One evening on my way home after a particularly difficult and frustrating day at the office, I found myself saying to God, "If You are real and can change a life, please change mine. Make me the kind of husband and father I ought to be. Forgive me for failing so badly."

I arrived home with a sense of peace and God's presence in my life that was a brand-new experience. That evening was quiet in our house as I mentally reviewed what had seemed to take place in the car. Along with an awareness of God's presence, I actually seemed to have a song in my

26

heart. *Surely,* I thought, *God has revealed Himself to me, or else I would not have this song, this quietness, in my life.*

The next morning I listened closely to the radio, and the words took on new significance. I left for work in a happy mood. Wondering if it was really God at work in my life, I hesitated to tell my family what had happened. Besides, I was not accustomed to communicating with them in a meaningful way.

After arriving home that evening, I announced, to everyone's surprise, that I was going to Sunday school and church with them next Sunday. What a stunned audience I had!

That Sunday morning, while Betty struggled getting the children ready, I did the dishes!

3

Forgiveness for a Full Life

"The thief comes only to steal, and kill, and destroy,"
Jesus exclaimed in John 10:10. "I came that they might
have life, and might have it abundantly." In my desperation I came to Jesus, the Great Physician. Years later one
of my sons, in his struggle for maturity, wrote in an article

for *Right On* that Jesus does His best work in the lives of desperate people.

To begin a new life, an alcoholic must first recognize his need for a higher authority than his own ego or self-control. In a sense we are all like the alcoholic, and our addiction is to self and sin. The chains of bondage are as firmly binding as those forged by alcohol, drugs and lesser bad habits. Anyone truly wanting help must first recognize his need for supernatural help.

Like most achievement-oriented men striving for power and position, I wanted to brag that I was self-sufficient, a power unto myself. My philosophy before my salvation could well have been described in the last quadrant of "Invictus," by W. E. Henley, "It matters not how straight the gate, how charged with punishment the scroll. *I* am the master of my fate, *I* am the captain of my soul" (italics added). Needless to say, when troubles came along, the god of self was too small!

Marriage brought problems with which I could not cope. Something had to give. I needed help, and lots of it! So out went the capital I, and in came Christ. As I confessed my need to Him and asked His forgiveness, I experienced, along with His peace and presence, a sense of forgiveness that is almost unexplainable.

LEARNING TO BE FORGIVEN

Prior to coming to Christ, I had accumulated a great load of guilt. Suddenly, as I confessed, the load was taken away. It actually seemed to affect me physically, in the sense that there was a new spring in my step. My eyes saw everything in a new light, as if I were gifted with new sight. Along with true conversion comes a change of attitude— toward God first, then toward our fellow man.

But I needed to learn more about forgiveness in order to

experience the fuller life Jesus promises to those who follow Him. God had already shown me in my drive toward business success and material gain my values were all wrong. Now He was ready to show me that forgiving was easy for Him because He loved me so much. Later, He showed me it is easy to forgive others when we first learn to love them.

GUILT TRANSFERENCE

God loved me so much He sent Jesus to die in my place, so that I could be free from my sin and guilt. God invented this system of guilt transference so I could live free from these unwelcome thought intruders and live a more abundant life.

Ever since God provided the way that leads to freedom of thought and peace of mind, man has been trying to sidestep it. Much psychotherapy seeks to find a person to blame for one's problems, and then transfers blame to the unsuspecting person—generally a mother or father who should have done better.

God's perfect solution of putting our guilt on Jesus also includes the perfect system of confession and cleansing. As we confess our sins, He can be depended on to forgive us and to cleanse us from every wrong. And it is perfectly proper for God to do this for us because Christ died to put away our sins (1 John 1:9).

More recently, psychiatrists, notably Mowrer and Glasser, have used the theories of confession and cleansing in their work, but have omitted the necessity of confessing to God through Christ. Their substitute for this is to have their patients confess to them or to a close friend or relative. But there is no substitute god big enough to forgive sin.

When I came to God, I was hurting so much from following humanistic ways, blaming all my troubles on my mother and father, as well as my children and wife. I was so sensitive that I nursed any fancied or real hurt until the mole-hill became a mountain.

In my frequent periods of bitter recrimination, I gave my wife the silent treatment. In many instances she was not even aware why I was angry. Each quarrel or silent period added to my problem of deep bitterness. I became a first-class bookkeeper against my wife. The Bible says, love "thinketh no evil" (1 Corinthians 13:5, KJV). In the Greek, "thinketh no evil" is actually a bookkeeping term, and means "taking into account no thought of evil."

When my wife and I got into an argument, I could open up the ledger books against her with computer speed and spew out the undesirable entries. There is nothing unusual about this behavior. It is not aberrant. This is happening in the world around us. It is the natural thing for husbands and wives to do.

Learning to Forgive Others

Men, are you keeping books against your wife? Now that you are forgiven by Christ (I am assuming you have asked Him to come into your life and forgive you), are you still unwilling to forgive your wife? It does not seem possible that we are willing to accept the forgiveness of God and not extend it to those closest to us.

God's teaching on forgiveness is plain. But where is the practice of it? Paul exhorts us, "I urge you therefore, brethren, by the mercies of God, to present your bodies a living and holy sacrifice, acceptable to God, which is your spiritual service of worship. And do not be conformed to this world, but be transformed by the renewing of your mind, that you may prove what the will of God is, that which is good and acceptable and perfect" (Romans 12:1-2).

Learning to forgive is part of learning to live the abundant life in Christ. He has much to say on the subject of forgiveness, including the fact that if we refuse to forgive others, He cannot forgive us (Matthew 6:15; 18:35; Mark 18:35). Peter was curious about the number of times we should forgive. He asked, " 'Lord, how often shall my brother sin against me and I forgive him? Up to seven times?' Jesus said to him, '. . . seventy times seven' " (Matthew 18:21-22).

Paul exhorts us, "Let all bitterness and wrath and anger and clamor and slander be put away from you, along with all malice. And be kind to one another, tender-hearted, forgiving each other, just as God in Christ has forgiven you. Therefore be imitators of God, as beloved children; and walk in love, just as Christ also loved you, and gave Himself up for us, an offering and a sacrifice to God as a fragrant aroma (Ephesians 4:31—5:2).

Many husbands complain of having wives who nag them to death. Thank God for that nagging wife (1 Thessalonians 5:18). Think of her as God's instrument to teach you patience and love that is not easily provoked. By all means point out to her, in love, that she is nagging. But forgive readily, seventy times seven if necessary.

Don't be bitter against your wife or hold a grudge against her for any reason. Peter said, "You husbands likewise, live with your wives in an understanding way, as with a weaker vessel, since she is a woman; and grant her honor as a fellow-heir of the grace of life, so that your prayers may not be hindered" (1 Peter 3:7).

Do not build an invisible wall between you and your mate because of some hurt or burden you are carrying. It is difficult to be in someone's presence when you encumber yourself with some real or fancied grievance. Learn to talk about your problems together, and learn to forgive as you have been forgiven. A happy marriage is a union between two forgivers.

LEARNING TO SAY "I'M SORRY"

Learning to say "I'm sorry" was such a major problem in the lives of one couple, that, they decided on a plan to solve it. Every time there were hurt feelings or bitterness, and quarrelsome words ensued, they would go into their bedroom and kneel by the bedside. They would tell each other they were sorry and ask forgiveness. Together they would pray about the problem over which they had argued.

Pride keeps us from saying the magic words *I'm sorry*. Saying them is so difficult that the world has tried to sidestep it by saying, "Love is not having to say, 'I'm sorry.'" But God was teaching this couple differently. First, the wife would say she was sorry, and then the husband would say it. Then came more prayer. But when everything seemed all right, the husband would get right back up from his knees and resume the battle, blaming her all over again. The rug into the bedroom became a path of contrition.

Time wore on, and so did the rug! Suddenly one day he said to his wife, "Honey, do you know that it's been almost a month since we made a trip into the bedroom for the 'I'm sorry' ritual?" He should not have mentioned it—later in the day they found it necessary to go in one more time.

Through many difficult situations, this couple learned to talk out their problems and say "I'm sorry," and to forgive and mean it. Through these learning situations, they finally achieved a sense of deeper love that drew them, as husband and wife, into God-ordained oneness.

Now they recall with a sense of happy humor the many quarrels, conflicts, and misunderstandings through which they worked in order to be joined together more deeply in love.

33

Reull Howe, in his book *The Miracle of Dialogue,* says, "The fruits of the Spirit are not achieved in a vacuum. They are achieved and found in the context of human relationships. We look there for the fruits of the Spirit."[1] Now this couple has a sense of being more deeply in love than ever before, because love is the number one fruit of the Spirit.

If you are having difficulty forgiving your wife read *The Freedom of Forgiveness,* by David Augsburger. It has helped many find release from bitterness and an unforgiving spirit.

4

Whom Do You See in the Mirror?

It has been a long path from the painful years of my homeless childhood to the present happiness and security of a home with a loving wife and four children. There were few bright spots in my struggle to grow up and become an adult. The only person in the entire world that meant anything to me was my sister, who was one year older than I. Though we were more often separated than together, we spent two years together in a home for deserted children. Later, we kept in touch by letters and occasional visits.

My mother and father were married at the onset of World War I and lived together long enough to bring my sister and me into the world. From that point on, they were adult delinquents. Temporarily we were pawns between them in the power struggle of their divorce and settlement. Neither of them had learned to cope with life, and both sought escape from its heavy responsibilities in various ways. Mother, who won the struggle for possession of us children, immediately sought ways of dispossessing herself by putting us in the custody of boardinghouse operators.

Then, as her life became involved with men and misfortune, she followed our father in becoming a dropout. We became wards of the court and residents of the Girls' and Boys' Aid Society home.

GROWING-UP PROBLEMS

Being unwanted and unloved brings hurts that do not heal, scars that persist, crushing loneliness, and defiling bitterness. Along the way, the death of my sister further embittered me. Of course, I blamed it all on my parents. It was the natural thing to do. But it added to my difficulties as I entered my early adult years with no advantage except an aggressive determination to do it all differently from my mother and father.

When my sister and I were in the children's home, we often sang, "Oh, if I had the wings of an angel, over these prison walls I would fly." We talked and wondered about God, but concluded He did not care about children, or He would have helped us in our needs.

Later, my sister and I were in various foster homes and

occasionally visited one another. We shared our hard, lonely experiences in childish self-sympathy, thinking we were two of the saddest, most miserable children in the world. We used to write stories about our eventual liberation from our troubles. But the liberation we sought and the happy endings we dreamed about were of the fairy tale, fairy godmother type. God seemed too distant to help us.

In the meantime, my mother was going her own way, trying to cope with the hardships of life. God was not in her thinking, either. Her hope seemed to be in snaring a husband who would take care of her and who might even be interested in assuming her two offspring. She came on and off the stage of our lives at strange intervals. For one short, disastrous period she rescued us from the grip of the legal authorities. We were in our early teens, and living with an alcoholic stepfather was beyond our ability to cope with. The situation directly contributed to the early death of my sister.

At an early age I was an embittered cynic, knowing far too much of all the wrong things in life. Well, if parents are not able to care for you, and you do not think God is around to help, what can you expect from the impersonal lap of public welfare? I never blamed them for all my problems, but heaped blame on my parents and hated God for allowing it all to happen.

As I was growing up I used to say, "Man, I'm never going to take the road my parents took. I'm never going to live their kind of lives!" I meant it, too. But the long path of life seems to lead irresistibly downward, and good resolutions and high standards set by young idealists are impossible for human attainment. So I inevitably lowered my standards, trying to set something manageable and achievable to bolster an inferiority complex and a terrible self-image.

No wonder so many young people get into trouble with crime, alcohol, drugs, and other aids and abetments to juvenile delinquency. Nobody seems to care. Self-pity, cynicism, and bitterness take a terrible toll from one's life. From such early experiences one is lucky to escape with any feeling of self-worth or value.

So many good things have been written on self-image, self-acceptance, and self-recognition that I hesitate to write more on this overworked but still generally misunderstood subject. Loving and unconditionally accepting oneself as God's unique person is basic to good mental health and sound relationships. "At the root of most problems," declares one psychologist, "is a poor self-image." Another one writes, "A good self-concept is more important than a college education."

Self-Image Problems

As we grow up, having "No! No!" hurled at us from birth through early maturity tends to program us negatively. Hard-to-endure events of life crush us and diminish our feelings of self-worth. Teen years are crisis years. The identity crisis through which so many of our youth pass results from a lack of self-acceptance and self-recognition. Fear of physical encounter with the opposite sex often leads to sex play and experimentation with those of one's own sex. Following experimentation, wrong sex habits may develop, which, when ingrained, lead to further identity problems compounded with guilt feelings and personality aberration. When ardent, youthful emotions become so involved, there is little or no objective thinking.

Even becoming a Christian may contribute to self-image problems. A mistaken notion that we become "nothing" when we ask Christ into our lives leads to self-demeaning, self-abnegating attitudes. Usually these forms of self-denial are phoney as we belittle ourselves publicly. We may not even believe what we are saying. Nonetheless, these self-paralyzing attitudes reveal our lack of self-worth.

As we Christians work and rub elbows daily with non-Christians, we find ourselves unable to enjoy the satisfaction of being accepted and understood in their world. In fact, we are often misunderstood, even ridiculed and rejected. Therefore our self-acceptance and self-respect can be greatly reduced. That is why it is so vitally necessary for Christians to be constantly in fellowship with one another in an accepting and understanding way. We need to encourage one another, understand and accept each other as persons. Sometimes the problem is finding a body of believers who will open their arms in an accepting and understanding way to everyone with Christlike love, helping to build others even as they are being built up themselves.

More Problems

Marriage creates further problems of self-worth. One of the major problems of marriage is the conflict of egos, each wanting his own way. From this two-party competition in the home emerges a victor, be it husband or wife. The one who loses the battle of the egos suffers loss of pride and self-respect, which can lead to such self-doubt that neurosis is the result. From the lost battle of the sexes emerges the henpecked husband or the whining, neurotic, defeated housewife.

When the husband loses the battle, he loses all self-respect. In his wrong role of submission to his wife, he may develop behavior problems. He chooses silence, for example, rather than being constantly cut down by his overbearing, dominant wife. In groups, his only timid venture into conversation results in contradictions and refutations by his aggressive mate. Rather than repeatedly face the embarrassments of his early experience, he becomes a "yes, love" personality, dishonored in the eyes of his fellow man and, worse yet, of his family.

The wife who wins the battle of the egos becomes more and more overbearing and dominant, so that her own personality is warped and dehumanized. Her matriarchal conduct affects her friends, relatives, and particularly her children, who ultimately suffer the most.

Just as serious a problem develops in the home when the husband wins the battle of the egos. From this relationship develops the meek woman with the neurotic whine. When her aggressive husband finally pressures her into complete submission, her self-worth disappears, and she becomes a broken woman with sadness and defeat written all over her countenance.

Even the battles themselves cause us to lose our self-respect. Slinging four letter words at one another deepens our dislike for ourselves as well as our mates. Eugene O'Neil said, "You cannot build a marble palace out of mud."

Nothing so humiliates a man or woman as divorce. Often the hurt endured by a sensitive man or woman resulting from a dissolved marriage destroys self-confidence and self-value.

The woman is likely to suffer most from a divorce. Many girls, brought up in the church and indoctrinated with Christian marriage-ethics, are taught that it is the wife who must give until it hurts. When such a marriage fails, the wife is most likely to see it as entirely her fault. Imagine the bruised, crushed ego and self-loathing that result from such guilt feelings!

I believe our divorce statistics today reflect the overcompensation of women who desire to be people leading worthwhile, fulfilled lives. Women trying to overcome

41

guilt feelings because of broken homes attempt to establish themselves as creatures of worth. Politicians, social workers and others are aiding their cause, sometimes for selfish reasons.

It Takes a Good Husband to Make a Good Wife

Men, we have the responsibility of healing our wives. We need to help them recover from hurts that may go back many years. But we can help them only when we develop a self-image free of selfishness. Then we can follow Christ's command to "love your neighbor [wives are neighbors] as yourselves" (Matthew 19:19) .

We need much help in this area before we can help our wives. God has given me this kind of help. Not only have I experienced what I am writing about, but in my own hurting there has been much healing. Now I want to pass this on to men who are interested in this healing process.

Although there are only a few authors offering books with practical help for men who want to live happily with the wives God has given them, there is a surfeit of books for women. Many of these writers place the responsibility for a happy home on the wife. Some women are being crushed by this burden of responsibility, for God never intended them to assume it.

Perhaps these writers of women's books have some partial solutions. But many of their principles, if used, fail to build a wife into a real person in the image of God and in oneness with her husband and the Almighty. Instead, they tend to construct a man-pleasing model bent on satisfying the husband at any cost. Sex seems to be the most important tool in the arsenal of wiles and guiles to subdue husbands.

I'm not against a wife desiring to satisfy her husband's needs. This gratification is very important to most men. However, if all her efforts are expended to satisfy her husband's fleshly appetites, it won't do anything for him as a man.

There is something unreal about a wife trying to play a role for which she is unsuited. Nor is it good for a wife to strive for happiness by becoming an obsequious slave. If God had wanted her to be her husband's slave, His Word would not say, "Be subject to one another in the fear of Christ" (Ephesians 5:21). He would have included instructions for wives under chapter six of Ephesians, where He gives instruction to slaves. However, the role of a wife is not mentioned here.

Some men would do well to treat their wives as well as they are exhorted to treat slaves. Even this would be a great improvement! Our wives are not slaves. We just treat them that way sometimes. They have been set free by the Lord Jesus Himself! Regarding this, the Bible says, "There is neither Jew nor Greek, there is neither slave nor free man, there is neither male nor female; for you are all one in Christ Jesus" (Galatians 3:28).

A wife who pursues the role of a sexual plaything to manipulate her husband only helps reinforce her husband's self-centeredness, putting him in further bondage to himself, and even to her. The man, by the wise design of our Creator, is normally the aggressor. He is the pursuer, and the wife is the pursued. Of course, this does not rule out the happy wife's being the occasional pursuer. She will have no fear of a husband who truly loves her! Yet it follows that the naturally aggressive wife must learn to exercise godly self-control, just as the naturally aggressive husband needs to exercise restraint.

I am quite sure that if a wife becomes the kind of person she ought to be and God wants her to be, this will increase the husband's loving response to her. Yet, it is the husband's God-given responsibility to love his wife as himself and to do it unconditionally, regardless of her responses. As a husband learns to love his wife unconditionally, it will overcome fear and insecurity in her life.

If you want to know where your wife and you stand in this matter of self-image, try this exercise: Take a three-by-five card or sheet of notepaper, and write five of your wife's good qualities on it. Take another card and write five of your good qualities on it. Let your wife do the same thing. Then compare notes.

Perhaps you will learn some surprising things about yourselves. If your children are old enough, do this exercise with them. You will see that you are all creatures of special worth. If the results are negative, you will know you are in need of special help. You can get this from God, God's Word, your pastor, and others qualified to assist.

It may be that you have some difficulty accepting yourself or your wife because of a physical feature, such as a large nose. Learn to give thanks for these supposed shortcomings. We are exhorted, "In everything give thanks; for this is God's will for you in Christ Jesus" (1 Thessalonians 5:18). Each of us is God's unique creation. Unless you accept the design, how can you accept the Designer?

BUILDING YOUR SELF-IMAGE

When your will is lined up with God's, you will not have major self-image problems. And when you begin to provide the right kind of leadership for your wife and family, you will be providing security for them by the person you are, not by what you provide materially.

Take inventory of yourself. What do you picture when you think of someone you know? Do you first think of their possessions and achievements—or the kind of person they are? What is your initial thought when meeting someone new? Is it, *I wonder what he thinks of me?* Or is it, *What is his need? How can I help him?*

Whom do you see in the mirror? "For as he thinks within himself, so he is," declares the writer of Proverbs (Proverbs 23:7). Do you see one who is unable to cope with life and its heavy responsibilities? Are you willing to let your wife bear all the responsibility and burden of raising the family and trying to make you happy? Have you been an unwanted, unloved child unwilling to accept accountability for your own life—all too willing to point the finger of blame at anyone but yourself?

Are you negative, critical, and judgmental as a result of an oppressed childhood or failures in early life? Or are you an embittered cynic with a defeated outlook on life? One unhappy friend of mine is so cynical! When I asked him what had led to his pessimistic outlook on life, he had a one word reply: "Disillusionment."

Disillusionment! Thank God for it. The loss of our illusions means the dawn of a new day of reality. Welcome disillusionment as a friend, and optimistically embark on a new adventure into life as it really is with God.

Have you lost the battle to your wife in the conflict of egos that takes place in every home at the beginning of marriage? Or have you domineered until your wife has lost her identity? Is yours a dominion of love or tyranny? No matter what the answer is, you can begin to construct a life that is worthwhile. You can become a person who knows his worth by fulfilling the role for which God created you. Accept the healing He wants to give you, and your life will be enriched and fulfilled as you accept the place of leadership and responsibility that is rightfully yours. Learn to accept yourself just as God made you, and then press on!

5

Abdicated Leadership

If in reading this far you have come to the conclusion that I put the responsibility for attaining a happy marriage on the husband, you are right! You and I, modern men, have tended to abdicate our true responsibility in our unrelenting search for success of one kind or another. But our only success has been in tossing the whole load of family leadership into the lap of our wives.

We have abdicated our God-given role, and we are now paying the price. Women have had to assume such a load of responsibility in the family, that now many are willing to bear it all, *without* a husband as part of their burden.

A Matriarchal Society

We may be heading for a matriarchal society unless we get back to fulfilling our husband-wife roles according to God's plan—not our own. Few men assume the spiritual responsibility that is theirs, under God's direction, to guide and instruct their families properly. The husband is no longer thought of as important to the home. In many circles, he has become the butt of humiliating jokes and the object of scorn by those who should be closest to him. The father-authority caricature in so many families is the root of much bitterness and resentment in children and young adults. This leads to further breakdown of the traditional family.

The True Example

Spiritual leadership, as ordained by God, is rooted in a paradox. Our Lord said, "If anyone wants to be first, he shall be last of all, and servant of all!" (Mark 9:35). Jesus demonstrated this best by washing the feet of His disciples.

Jesus set the example and gave us the principle in Scripture. We are not to domineer our wives, demanding they submit to our leadership. Jesus said, "You know that those who are recognized as rulers of the Gentiles lord it over them; and their great men exercise authority over them. But it is not so among you, but whoever wishes to become great among you shall be your servant; and whoever wishes to be first among you shall be slave of all. For even the Son of Man did not come to be served, but to serve, and to give his life a ransom for many" (Mark 10:42-45).

Husbands should have the attitude described by Paul, "Have this attitude in yourselves which was also in Christ Jesus, who, although He existed in the form of God, did not regard equality with God a thing to be grasped, but emptied Himself, taking the form of a bond-servant, and being made in the likeness of man. And being found in appearance as a man, He humbled Himself by becoming obedient to the point of death, even death on a cross" (Philippians 2:5-8).

Is your love for your wife so evident that you are helping her become the kind of wife God wants her to be? Are you her spiritual head, leading her in family prayer and devotions so as to make her holy and clean through the use and application of God's Word?

In our nearly matriarchal society, it is no wonder women automatically recoil at the thought of man as the head of the woman. One author writes, "Much of what women have seen of this headship has been destructive and tyrannical. This dominance is a perversion of the masculine headship which is supposed to be a dominion of love rather than a dominion of tyranny. True love is a power that nurtures and serves, rather than one that dominates. The one who rules in the spiritual sense, as Christ taught, is the one who becomes least by serving."[1]

LEADING OUR WIVES

Where are the men who are willing to give the leadership God has commanded us to provide? Just saying "I'm boss" or "I'm the head of this house" doesn't make it so. Dr. Howard Hendricks, professor at Dallas Theological Seminary, says, "We never learn to lead until we know what leadership involves. You are not a leader by virtue of your title—but on the basis of your performance."[2]

Becoming a leader involves learning to be one. Some leaders may be born, some may have leadership thrust upon them, but most leaders are made. If you are married, you have had leadership thrust upon you by the commitment of your marriage vows. If you have not learned how to lead, do not despair. It is never too late to start.

It was very difficult for me to become a leader, first, in business; second, in our church; third, in our home; and last, in the Campus Crusade movement. I am not recommending the above order; it just worked out that way for me. Actually, leadership in the home comes first by God's commandment. The home is also where it counts the most. If you can learn to be a leader in your home, you will, in the process, become a better leader everywhere else.

A leader, by Webster's definition, is: "one who leads or guides, one who shows the way or directs the course of another." A leader is one who is able to convince others they should go along with him. He must have clear-cut objectives and be highly motivated.

A leader must have followers. Initially these should be the members of his family. A leader must have deep, personal commitment, first to the Lord Jesus and then to his cause—in this case, his family. A family leader must maintain a worthwhile schedule, with his priorities well in line.

Leadership demands self-denial. It means taking up the cross of Christ and following Him. You won't be able to follow Him unless you begin to learn what His Word says to you. Leadership essentially involves the will. A man is capable of leadership when he sets a reasonable goal then presses on with all he has toward it. A leader in the home must be able to make decisions and carry them out. Like

49

Paul, he needs to learn how to say, "This one thing I do"—not "These fifty things I dabble in"! (Philippians 3:13, KJV).

A leader must have that attitude of mind and heart that Paul expressed: "Brethren, I do not regard myself as having laid hold of it yet; but one thing I do: forgetting what lies behind and reaching forward to what lies ahead, I press on toward the goal for the prize of the upward call of God in Christ Jesus" (Philippians 3:14).

As you "press on" to reach the end of the race of life, take your wife and family with you—not by forcing them, but by inspiring them.

6

The Successful Man

What qualities would you like to have in order to be a successful business or professional man? Your answer might include intelligence, a well-disciplined life, complete commitment and dedication to the pursuit of a cause, or persuasiveness and leadership.

52

Or would you rather have the qualities that lead to being a successful family man? Would you like to have a good education on family life, with input from recognized authorities? Would you like to be a well-organized person who knows where he is leading his wife and family? Would you choose complete commitment to the pursuit of a happy life, wife and family? Are you a persuader and leader in your home? Can a man be successful both in business and in his family? My experience, having founded a chain of six retail stores and co-founded a wholesale electrical supply company, has proven to me that the attitudes and involvement of the successful businessman today substantially lessen one's chances of being a good husband and father.

The successful businessman, professional man, and in many cases, clergyman, must be enamored with his work to the extent that it is business in the morning, at noontime and in the evening. His thoughts are centered on his chosen field of endeavor even when he is home with his family. He is willing to discipline himself for the sake of his vocation. Not only is he willing to be the first one on the job in the morning, but he is also willing to be the last to leave.

If you are a man in this category, what do you have left to give your family each evening when you get home? You arrive there physically and emotionally drained. You may know God wants you to be the leader in your home. You may know He holds you responsible for the spiritual welfare of your wife and children. But you have nothing to give. You are spent. Instead of being able to minister to others as you should, you want to be ministered to. Instead of giving your family the things they need and expect from a husband and father, your life becomes centered on self, and your role becomes one of getting from other family members instead of giving. You give all you have at work, so there is nothing left to give at home.

What does the world of industry and commerce expect of its men on the job? Everything! The more capable a man is, the more there is expected from him. The higher his position in the world, the greater the responsibilities and the greater the demands on his time and talents. Many companies, particularly large corporations, expect the wife to fit in and adapt to their demands on her husband. Some corporations actually interview the wives of prospective executive talent.

WORKING WIVES

To add burden to burden in the home, nearly 50 percent of today's wives are working. When the work-weary husband and wife arrive home from the day's labor, and he asks her to perform in the kitchen, her attitude may be, "Wait on yourself, brother, I've been working all day, too," or, "Forget it. I'm beat!"

I am not against working wives, or I should say, wives that are working on outside jobs. Certainly there are circumstances in which wives are forced to work. God may even call a woman to outside work, but not at the expense of the husband and children. Because of the way God has made them, women can still find their greatest fulfillment in their homes and communities. Their talents and abilities can usually be expressed in many ways without outside employment.

When the traditional husband-wife relationship is confused by a working wife or mother, home life can become barely tolerable, and many times the children or the wife, with their own desperate needs, cannot long endure such an arrangement. Soon there may be trouble with truant children and even worse problems. Working wives, no longer able to cope with such overwhelming circumstances, are

54

today leaving their husbands in alarming numbers, and the divorce courts are busier than ever.

When a wife walks out on her husband, suddenly his job, profession or business seems to lose its glamour. In time of such family trauma, the importance of a job becomes questionable. Where is his priority now? Is it still going to be business as usual?

You've Got It All

So, you've got the best mattress in town, the best money can buy! But if you can't relax on it or sleep on it, what good is it? It is better to have a lumpy mattress and a fulfilled relationship with your wife than the best mattress from the most fashionable department store!

So, you have the biggest and best car available; but is it carrying around the most miserable man in town? It is better to have a used Volkswagen and happiness and peace in your family than to have the finest wheels Detroit can provide and be miserable. Cruising around the country in a Rolls is beautiful only if you're "rolling along, singing a song" because there is peace in your heart.

So, yours is one of the best homes on the block or maybe in the city. But if there is a brawling couple inside, I am sure you would gladly exchange it for a quiet cottage with love and harmony. Tranquility in the home makes the modest dwelling a bit of heaven.

Among the many "things" a man may treasure are a yacht, a sixteen-foot boat and trailer, a camper, an airplane and other status symbols. There is certainly nothing wrong with a man having a few men's toys. C. S. Lewis, famous Christian writer said, "God loves material things; He made them." But it is where your heart is that counts.

As men struggle to get and retain their share of life's good things, they always want more. And then, after getting more and still more, they experience the empty frustration of trying to keep up with everybody, keep up with everything, and keep everything up. And most men wonder, after each new acquisition, if there isn't something more to life than all these "things?"

From time to time men come to me hopeless and depressed. They have lost their zest for living. Their nights may be sleepless and their days an intolerable drag. Some, in their desire for money and success, are, financially speaking, stretched out to the breaking point. They think money is their only problem! Others seem to have it all put together financially, but the boredom of their lives in their business, professional or working world is driving them crazy. But they are forced to go on and on because of their established standard of living and the insatiable desire for more.

Some who have not made it but still want to are encumbered with bitterness toward those who, they imagine, stood in their way in their pursuit of the dollar and the glamour of success. Some seek escape from the "locked-in" or "trapped" feeling by doing things that only lead to deep guilt and deeper unhappiness.

Yes, what good are successes, achievements in the realm of "things," when values are materialistic and goals temporal? Unless goals are determined by eternal values, life will suffer from an indescribable emptiness. It will become meaningless, and every pursuit of life will be a dead-end street. Such a condition can lead to alienation from friends and family.

Paul, the great apostle, as he relates God's anger toward men who push away the truth, describes our emptiness in the following fashion: "For the truth about God is known to [men] instinctively; God has put this knowledge in their hearts" (Romans 1:19). To paraphrase St. Augustine, we were made for God, and we are restless until we find our rest in Him.

The Lord Jesus had much to say about a rich man whose possessions became so numerous, he did not have room for them all. The rich man made a decision that any board of directors would have approved. He decided to build bigger warehouses in which to store all his things (Luke 12:16-29). But God reprimanded him for his confused priorities.

The Lord said you cannot take possessions with you when you die. Furthermore, treasures for yourself mean little if you are not rich toward God. There is more to life than material things, "For all these things do the nations of the world seek after; and your Father knoweth that ye have need of these things. But rather seek ye the kingdom of God; and all these things shall be added unto you. . . . For where your treasure is, there will your heart be also" (Luke 12:30-31, 34, KJV).

Would you believe that the knowledge and skills you have acquired in your job, business or profession are the very ingredients you will need, if you really want a success-ful marriage and want to become the kind of husband and father God wants you to be? Just as the responsibility for a good business rests on the president, and the responsibility for a good military unit rests on the commander-in-chief, so the responsibility for the home unit and the family rests on the husband.

Singleminded Men

Benjamin Disraeli, one of England's greatest prime min-isters, said, "The secret of success is constancy of purpose." Jesus said, "If . . . thine eye be single, thy whole body shall be full of light" (Matthew 6:22, KJV). He was saying, "Be a single-eyed person." The Bible also reminds us, "A double-minded man is unstable in all his ways (James 1:8, KJV).

Life consists of many hard choices. Only the single-minded man will be able to make the right ones. The truly committed man has his eyes on the things of eternal value. In the parable of the sower, Jesus tells us the seed that fell among thistles is the man who hears the word [the Good News], and the worry of the world and the deceitfulness of riches choke the word, and it becomes unfruitful" (Matthew 13:22). Jesus said, "Stop toiling for the food that perishes, but toil for the food that lasts for eternal life, which the Son of Man will give you, for God the Father has given Him authority to do so" (John 6:27, Williams).

PRIORITIES

Are you longing for earthly riches or eternal life? Are you yearning for financial security and possessions, or are you seeking first the kingdom of God? (Matthew 6:33). Where are your priorities? There is nothing wrong with money, and I do not want to give the impression I think there is. But when money is the goal of our ambition and desire, then we are wrongly motivated.

Are you consumed with selfish ambition, which, according to James, leads to "disorder and every evil thing (3:16)? Or are you seeking the wisdom that comes from heaven and is "first pure, then peaceable, gentle, reasonable, full of mercy and good fruits" (3:17).

Wisdom (the use of knowledge and experience) is more greatly to be desired than riches. "How blessed is the man who finds wisdom, and the man who gains understanding. For its profit is better than the profit of silver, and its gain than fine gold. She is more precious than jewels; and nothing you desire compares with her" (Proverbs 3:13-15).

58

"Some rich people are poor," another proverb tells us, "and some poor people have great wealth" (13:7, TLB). It all depends on our viewpoint and value system. The man who puts God first, the family second and his business or profession third, may find it harder to succeed in this world. However, his priorities will bring blessing from God, and his earthly rewards will be the happiest kind.

7

Make Love Your Aim

The man who does not aim at something will miss everything. So make love your aim—unconditional love, not "if" or "because" love. "If" love says, "I'll love you *if* you respond to me the way I want you to." Or, "I'll love you *if* you never disagree with me." "Because" love says, "I love

60

you *because* you're such a good cook." Or, "I love you *because* you are so beautiful."

Love is an attitude of heart and mind. It begins with a spirit of thankfulness. If yours is an ungrateful, unthankful attitude, perhaps you do not have a right relationship with the Lord Jesus Christ. Coming to Him involves repentance, a change of attitude. To repent, defines Webster, is "to change one's mind with regard to past or intended action, conduct, etc., on account of regret or dissatisfaction."

To make love your aim, you must have this spirit of wanting to do things differently. You may need an earnest desire to again win your wife. This longing must be accompanied by a new attitude toward God, your marriage, your wife, and your children.

A Right Understanding

A reorientation of your thinking is not enough. It must be coupled with a right understanding, which can come only from knowing God's Word. Proverbs exhorts us to get wisdom, or a right understanding: "Happy is the man that findeth wisdom, and the man that getteth understanding" (3:13, KJV).

The Bible also admonishes, "You husbands also, live with your wives in an understanding way, as with a weaker vessel, since she is a woman; and grant her honor as a fellow-heir of the grace of life, so that your prayers may not be hindered" (1 Peter 3:7).

We are also instructed, "Always give thanks for everything to our God and Father in the name of our Lord Jesus Christ" (Ephesians 5:20). One thing that helped me in changing my attitude toward my wife was daily practicing an attitude of thanksgiving for her.

Along with practicing thanksgiving I recognized I had to display a lighthearted, happy spirit. The Bible says we are

61

to "Rejoice evermore!" (1 Thessalonians 5:16, KJV). In spite of circumstances, you ask? No, *because* of circumstances. This two-word verse is a commandment from the Lord. Practice rejoicing, by faith, whether you feel like it or not. There is no better way to practice rejoicing than to practice a smile!

The most important thing is to make love your aim. By faith, *practice* loving your wife and your children (as well as your neighbors and friends). The apostle John gives us these important instructions on how to love by faith: "Beloved, let us love one another, for love is from God; and everyone who loves is born of God and knows God. The one who does not love does not know God, for God is love" (1 John 4:7-8).

If you will obey God and begin to practice loving by faith, then you will begin to have the right feelings. Your tomorrows will be as bright as the promises of God. "Obedience to His will today means that God assumes the responsibility of our tomorrow," says Charles L. Allen in *God's Psychiatry.*"[1]

SOME WIVES ARE SMARTER

A happy marriage develops when you learn to ask your wife's opinion on everything. What a shock it is for many men to find that their wives are smarter than they! Some men crumble under this discovery. Others, filled with resentment, refuse to believe the truth, and bully their way along, insisting that the wife has no right to be a thinking member of the family. Men, if you discover your wife is smarter than you, capitalize on it. Begin to share all your brain-straining problems with her. Ask her opinion on everything. She will love you for it.

People love to give their opinions. Begin to weigh her opinions, and compare them with yours if there is a difference. Use her opinions on some matters, no matter how insignificant they seem. And be sure to tell her, "Honey, that was a whale of an idea you gave me." You will begin to earn her respect, admiration, and recognition for your discernment. She may even begin to suspect you are the smarter one!

DYING TO SELF

To begin this program, you must learn to say to self, "Drop dead!" Jesus said, "Except a corn of wheat fall into the ground and die, it abideth alone; but if it die, it bringeth forth much fruit" (John 12:24, KJV). Think of the rewards of such a strategy as this. Communication lines between you and your wife will open up as never before.

LEARNING TO AIM AT GOD'S LOVE

The Bible says that all we need is "faith working through love" (Galatians 5:6). Shortly after I became a Christian, God taught me some important things about His love. He taught me through His Word, teachers, and preachers, and especially through my family, how I could demonstrate this love to others by faith.

Following my conversion I took my family to a seaside resort town, where we rented a small cottage for a week. Nearby was Cannon Beach Conference Center, an interdenominational retreat where we went to hear various well-known Christian speakers.

On arriving at the beach, we settled in and had a happy weekend. The children played in the sand. Even the youngest, who was still in diapers, spent hours in his playpen out in the sun. In typical young-husband fashion, I viewed these moments of being alone with my wife as an opportunity to make "love" my aim.

In selfishness I overlooked the many hours of hard work

my wife had gone through preparing for the week, to say nothing of the constant drain on her energy while caring for a husband and family seven days a week. I had been little or no help to her because of my long hours of ambitious business climbing. So the usual frustrations attended my lovemaking efforts.

Sunday night, the conference speaker spoke on the subject "Make Love Your Aim." Surely, I thought, this would be something good for Betty and me—especially Betty. The Bible text from 1 Corinthians had a familiar ring, and I wondered where I had heard the expression. Soon I discovered, as I listened intently, the speaker was talking about a love of which I knew little or nothing—God's love, the kind that *gives* instead of *takes,* the kind that perseveres in the face of overwhelming obstacles.

Repetition the Best Teacher

After the meeting I said good-bye to my family and headed for Portland, about seventy-five miles inland, so I could be on the job early Monday morning. As I was driving along thinking of the problems in my life, I switched on the car radio. It was tuned to a late-night broadcast of Billy Graham's "Hour of Decision." His subject was love. I was surprised at this coincidence. I thought, *Oh no, not again,* but I decided to listen. The sermon was from the most important writing of all time on the subject of love, chapter thirteen of 1 Corinthians. The message included the phrase "make love your aim."

These words had a strange familiarity. Then the light switched on! My wife had spoken those words to me a long time ago, after one of our bitter struggles to make love. The entire conversation came back to my mind. "If you want sex with me in the evening, you've got to start in the morning. You've got to make love your aim in the morning."

64

*In the morning—in the morning—*the humming of the tires on the dry pavement seemed to reecho.

A New Life Attitude

From that night on, I began to make love my aim—God's love, the love that works by faith rather than by feelings. My new attitude began in the morning shower. I found myself singing. I began thanking my wife regularly for the good breakfast she always prepared for me. As a regular habit, I kissed her fondly before leaving for work.

Sure, I failed many times. There were times of morning irritability. Sometimes the morning parting included some bitter feelings and expressions. However, slowly but surely, we began to enjoy a better relationship, the fruit of practicing in a small way God's love, undeserved, unreserved, and unconditional.

Love From the Mouth of a Babe

One morning our baby daughter, Arlene, taught me a lesson about God's love that is written deeply on my heart. Arlene loved her daddy, and being an early riser, she was always at the table with me at breakfast. However, she was a baby girl with a tiny appetite. One of our major problems was getting her to eat. She was making her usual happy, childish noises, banging on the high chair tray with her silverware and at the same time ignoring the food in front of her.

In an impulsive moment of irritation I raised my voice and said, "For goodness' sake, Arlene, shut up and eat your breakfast!"

She looked stunned. Slowly a large tear, then another, formed and splashed on her tray. She began struggling to get out of her high chair, which she had just learned to do. She climbed down the side and came over next to me.

65

Reaching up with her tiny arms and pulling my ear down to her mouth, she said softly, "Daddy, I love you!"

I picked her up and responded with amazement. Yes, God was teaching me more about love, His love. The love Arlene showed me that morning was His kind of love—undeserved and unconditional. And it brought a loving response.

The "First Loving" Principle

This is God's principle of "first loving." The Bible declares, "We love him, because he first loved us" (1 John 4:19, KJV). Yes, we love because He first loved us. When we begin practicing first loving others by faith, whether we feel like it or not, they respond. We need patience, however, because they may not respond immediately.

What a tremendous concept we have here! If you believe this and practice it on your wife, the spark of love will rekindle and then burst into flame. She will start being the wife you always wanted! Although I have been writing of God's love, this concept carries over into your sexual relationship. And your sexual love will expand into a fuller dimension than you have ever experienced. What a love affair you and your wife can have! It will grow with the years. Remember, divine transformation usually takes a little time, so be patient.

As I learned to consistently practice what I had learned, new progress in our husband-wife relationship began to show up. I found myself calling my wife at ten or so in the morning, sometimes earlier, asking her to forgive me for being argumentative at breakfast or for some other unkindness, such as giving her the silent treatment.

She began calling me for the same reasons. Occasionally I asked her to go to lunch or do some shopping with me, or I just called to tell her I loved her. New love was beginning to bud and blossom, God's love, shed abroad in my heart through the Holy Spirit (Romans 5:5). Love was beginning to be my aim and guide. I was beginning to love her in the morning, at noontime and in the evening.

Bitterness Defiles

Times of bitterness between us came less frequently. Much of my bitterness came because she still did not seem to be the lover I had imagined she would be when we were first married. Some of my bitterness and disappointment was a result of my own unrealistic expectations. My opportunistic thinking, like that of most men today, had been conditioned by Madison Avenue presentations and promotions on radio and television instead of by God and His Word. His Word is very explicit in telling how to use His love.

A recurring theme in today's world is "love is never having to say I'm sorry." This is a contradiction and escape from biblical truth. God's Word is very frank and instructive on the matter of forgiveness. Learning to say "I'm sorry" is nearly as important as learning how to use God's love. When you want someone to forgive you, you first need to say you are sorry. It indicates a change of attitude and has a wonderful, guilt-releasing and cleansing effect and prevents an accumulation of bitterness.

Paul writes, "Let all bitterness and wrath and anger and clamor and slander be put away from you, along with all malice. And be kind to one another, tender-hearted, forgiving each other, just as God in Christ also has forgiven you" (Ephesians 4:31-32).

There is no room for bitterness in the Christian home. Nothing kills love more than being angry for some imagined fault, slight, or hurt—and this affects every facet of our relationship.

67

God's Word exhorts us, "Pursue peace with all men, and the sanctification without which no one will see the Lord. See to it that no one comes short of the grace of God; that no root of bitterness springing up causes trouble, and by it many be defiled" (Hebrews 12:14-15).

Our God-ordained responsibility is to love our wives as Christ loved the Church and gave Himself for her (Ephesians 5:25). We are to love our wives whether or not they show love to us. Do you love your wife enough to die for her? True, this is a hypothetical question. None of us can say he would unless he is faced with the necessity. But we can learn to die to self in a way that means dying while we go on living. We can die to self-desire of every kind and put our wives ahead of ourselves, learning to serve them even as the Lord Jesus came to serve us.

We hurt ourselves most when we fail to be loving and kind toward our wives. When we harbor anger and bitterness toward them, we utterly defile ourselves. We can learn to say "I'm sorry" just as easily as "I forgive you." With God's help, we can learn to be kind and loving.

Make love your aim. You will get a forever reward!

8

You Won Her Before, Do It Again!

Have you lost that old glow? Have you lost your wife's love? You won her once—and you can do it again. You can win her by making love your aim. If she is not already a Christian you can win her to the Lord Jesus Christ by your good example and godly life. With His love showing in your life, and by using the sound mind God has given you, you can win her to a new, lasting relationship that transcends earthly love.

The kind of love that brings a man and woman together in marriage is great! It does the job God wants it to do. But unless you learn about His love and how to practice it in your daily life, you are either in trouble or headed in that direction. Hollywood-style love is a kind of glue, but it is not waterproof. When deep water comes, it will not hold the marriage together.

Many marriages that seem to survive on this superficial kind of love are only for convenience. There are millions of marriages that exist for the sake of economy and comfort. Many couples coexist by détente and have a relationship of quiet desperation.

The fact that the marriage is mixed may be one cause. Perhaps you were brought up in a Christian home, yet you ignored the warnings about a mixed marriage. When you and your girlfriend were making your "everlasting love" commitments, marrying a Christian seemed unimportant. Well, the one you wanted was the one you got, and right up to the wedding day, and perhaps for some time after, you could not understand why your parents were heartbroken.

Now, after six years or so of marriage and one or two children, much of the thrilling excitement of the early marriage has ebbed. Furthermore, you have discovered babies yell and smell, drool and pool. You both seem unable to cope, and you have endured all you can. Suddenly you realize you need a foundation for your marriage in order to give it some meaning and durability. Your Christian background gives you the sneaking suspicion that there is no foundation for marriage except that ordained by God. The Bible says, "For this cause a man shall leave his father and mother, and shall cleave unto his wife; and the two

71

shall become one flesh" (Ephesians 5:31). You realize you are not perfectly joined to your wife and there is little or no oneness between you.

If there is any communication between you, you may decide to be brave and see a pastor or marriage counselor to repair the damage and establish a foundation for an ongoing marriage. Now you are aware that the oneness of body you and your wife experienced in the early part of your marriage does not equal oneness of mind and heart. You desperately need something to hold your lives together.

Christ is no homebreaker. He is the greatest homemaker there is. He can make any home a bit of heaven if He is given the chance. It is our unbelief and selfish actions that often stand in the way.

You may be like my friend Bill (not his real name). Bill attended a Christian Businessmen's meeting a few years ago and responded to the invitation to receive Christ. He found that having Christ in his life was great for him, but it only seemed to drive a larger wedge between him and his wife and family. After a couple of years he began to wonder if losing his wife and children was the price God wanted him to pay for becoming a Christian.

When Bill became a Christian, he learned from the Bible that his wife was supposed to submit to his leadership and adapt to his way of life (1 Peter 3:1). But Bill had a wife who would not adapt. Consequently, he did not understand how to play his new role in a way pleasing to God and calculated to win his wife to Christ. Bill represents multiplied thousands of lonely Christian husbands who do everything wrong attempting to attract their wives to Jesus Christ.

How Not to Do It

Then one day when I attended a men's early-morning

breakfast and prayer meeting, I spied a seat next to Bill. I always enjoyed sitting next to him. We were like-minded in many ways. He was a businessman, as I had been before my full-time involvement with Campus Crusade for Christ. He was a zealot for Christ; so was I. The main difference between us was that some twenty years had elapsed since the day I asked Christ into my life, and only two years had gone by since Bill was saved.

Since coming to Christ, Bill's heart was heavy with concern for his wife. From the day of his salvation his wife was increasingly antagonistic toward the church and Bill's new religious friends. So this morning, as he did every week, Bill shared his burden for his wife's conversion. He described her latest antireligious feelings and her threat to leave him unless he gave up his Christian friends and activities. Obviously Bill was very upset.

Before the prayer meeting started, the men shared various prayer requests with each other. There were the usual ones: prayer for loved ones, sick ones, those suffering loss of loved ones, business problems and other burdens. Bill's usual weekly prayer request was for the conversion of his wife.

Most of us included Bill's wife in our prayers that morning. We pleaded with God to convert her; to make her see the error of her ungodly ways and bring peace to their home. We all sincerely wanted her to share in this wonderful, new life of Bill's. His desire for this, naturally, was far stronger than ours, and his own prayer was the most fervent.

After the prayer meeting, many of the men came over to Bill to offer condolences and to empathize with him over the strange ways of his errant wife. And Bill knowingly and sadly shook his head, accepting their pity with gratitude and mutterings, such as, "I just don't know what's wrong with her, anyway. Why doesn't she change?"

The men began breaking up to go to their jobs, and I lingered behind to walk out with Bill.

"Bill," I said, "have you ever thought of planning a strategy to win your wife to Christ?"

"No," he replied. "I just haven't got the slightest idea how I can help her or win her. If prayer won't work, I don't know what will!"

Then I told Bill how my own experience had been similar to his, in reverse, and how my wife had planned a strategy to win me. And because her plan involved faith and obedience to God's Word, it worked. My wife would be the first to say she used the strategy as God motivated her and provided the circumstances, without being overly conscious of implementing a plan or manipulating me in any way.

At the conclusion of my testimony I said to Bill, "Why don't we pray together and ask God to give you a plan to win your wife?"

We prayed briefly before we parted. During the day my mind continued to go back to our morning conversation. I knew of other men in Bill's position, and my heart was stirred with compassion for all of them.

The more I thought about Bill's situation, the more ideas seemed to pop into my head. I would like to share some of these with men whom I believe could win their wives not only to Christ, but also to themselves in the process. The starting place is to prayerfully seek a strategy from God and His Word. And then, the hardest part is to apply the strategy, prayerfully and in the power of God's Holy Spirit.

WHAT IS WRONG WITH YOUR WIFE?

I don't like to begin on a negative note. But men like Bill always describe the many things wrong with their wives. They include their worldly habits; their dislike of their husbands' newfound Christian friends; their resentment of their husbands' Christian activities such as attending Sunday morning and evening church, Wednesday evening prayer meeting, Christian Business Men's Committee, and other Christian functions. Even the children of these men are caught up in the family tug-of-war of Mom pulling against God, and Dad pulling toward Him. And God and men like Bill don't seem to be winning.

Then I remembered the wise counsel given to husbands and wives by my pastor years ago. At that time his remarks were especially directed to husbands and wives with non-Christian mates. "If you have become a Christian and your mate has not, *who* has changed?" he asked. Well, the answer obviously is, the Christian.

Here is the root of the problem. Men, you are a new creation in Christ, and you like what God is doing to His new creation. You like the liberation from your old self-centeredness, from your old enslaving habits, and from the unrest of a mind in constant turmoil. You like the new things God is doing slowly but surely in your life.

Your wife, however, is still the same person you married. You loved her then, didn't you? And don't you still love her? If you don't, it is because your love wasn't the real thing.

"Yes," you say, "I still love her. But I want her to share in this exciting new life God has given me. I want her to change, too." (And only you know how badly she needs changing!)

Perhaps you are like one man with whom my wife and I recently counseled. He said, "Well, I think I've lost my love for my wife. The way she acts and the things she has done have killed my love for her." If that is the case, cheer up. If you have lost your love for her, it was not genuine love in the first place. You cannot lose genuine love. If she

75

has killed your love, it was a love dependent on her—not God. You can learn to love her with God's love.

If you do not love your wife anymore, you can start learning now. Because we are commanded to love our wives, we need to develop and cultivate love, not human love, but God's *agape,* unconditional love. You can begin to practice it, whether you feel like it or not. The right feeling will come later (John 14:21).

Give yourself to your wife, even as God in Christ gave Himself to us; make her your prized possession even as we are the prized possessions of God. As He loves us, love her, even if she is an ungodly sinner and your enemy for the present. You are not called upon to judge her but to love and redeem her. If your wife is rebellious, ask God why. Ask *What's wrong with me?* You can only change yourself, so begin there.

The right kind of love is rooted in faith. The foundation is 1 Corinthians 13. Go the way of the cross by loving sacrificially. Any other way is a satanic substitute.

One of my sons wrote, "The 'rule' of love is like the influence of the sun over the earth. The sun does not force life and punish the ground; the sun nurtures the living creatures of the earth, flooding its rays on the animals and drawing the living plants up from the ground and into the perfection of their being."[1]

Unlike the law, love is not a force which coerces from without. Love is a power that persuades from within, transforming by His Word and the power of the Holy Spirit. These same principles of love can be used in winning your wife to yourself, as well as to the Lord Jesus.

We husbands often want to lay the law down to our wives and children. They may submit on the outside but rebel on the inside. If you are trying to play Moses in your home, cut it out! E. Karen Howe said "A man's home is not really a castle over which he presides in lordly sovereignty. In the beginning of his efforts to make it a truly Christian home it is more like Golgotha, where he dies to himself in order to meet the needs of others!"[2]

DOING YOUR OWN THING

Why is it that you, in your ardent desire for your wife to become a Christian, usually do the wrong thing? I believe it is because, as new Christians, *we* still do things our own way out of lack of information and misdirected zeal. *We* want to fellowship with our new Christian friends; *we* want to go to church and prayer meetings and all the Bible studies *we* can squeeze into our schedules because of our new hunger for God and His Word. But our non-Christian wives do not want to go with us to these religious functions any more than we wanted to go to them before we were saved. Remember, the Bible says, "But a natural man [one who is not a Christian] does not accept the things of the Spirit of God; for they are foolishness to him, and he cannot understand them, because they are spiritually appraised" (1 Corinthians 2:14).

You have spiritual insight, but this just bothers and baffles your wife, and she can't understand you at all (1 Corinthians 2:15). In her spiritual poverty, she deserves your deepest and warmest sympathy, rather than your critical, judgmental attitude. Whereas you are beginning to have the thoughts and mind of Christ, she is still spiritually uneducated.

You want to do the things you are now doing because they result in inner blessing and reward to yourself. But that is what is standing in the way of winning your wife to Christ. Essentially, as a new Christian, you are still doing your own selfish thing. You must give up your own desires to win your wife. You must be controlled by God's de-

77

sires, and He wants to win your wife to Christ through you. "The Lord is . . . not wishing for any to perish but for all to come to repentance" (2 Peter 3:9). God loves your wife so much that He sent Jesus to earth for her. Jesus loves her so much He was willing to die for her, even though she is ungodly and His enemy at this time. "But God demonstrates His own love toward us, in that while we were yet sinners, Christ died for us" (Romans 5:8).

So you see that while prayer for your wife is needful and good, you must bear in mind Peter's admonition: "You husbands likewise, live with your wives in an understanding way, as with a weaker vessel, since she is a woman; and grant her honor as a fellow-heir of the grace of life, so that your prayers may not be hindered" (1 Peter 3:7).

How to Do It

You won her before, you can do it again. You won her to the altar where all those sweet promises immortalized in thousands of love songs seemed on their way to fulfillment. With little or no planning you achieved your shortsighted goal, and now you want to get on with something else. Besides, you are a very busy man, and it took a lot of time to win her the first time!

Speaking of planning and goals, why is it that we men spend a minimum of twelve years planning and preparing for some type of job vocation and practically no time getting ready for a lifetime of marriage? No wonder we make so many mistakes. Everyone makes mistakes when he tries to do something for which he is untrained.

The Bible says you must be understanding of your wife and her needs (1 Peter 3:7). And that takes time. If you want a successful marriage (and the word *successful* means "resulting or terminating favorably or as desired"), you

78

have to put in some time working on it. Goals, planning, and preparation are indispensable.

Begin praying, "God, make me the kind of husband and father you want me to be. Help me win my wife again."

A Strategy to Win Your Wife

Now start planning a strategy to win your wife. The first principle is to deny self. You must give up your rights to do the things you want to do. This includes good things like prayer meetings and Bible studies, if necessary. Forsake your own desires. Unless we learn to die to self, we will never become fruitful.

You will not have to starve or die spiritually. You can study and pray privately, and even enjoy some fellowship at lunches with your pastor and Christian friends. But your fellowship must not arouse the wrath of your wife. You must develop an attitude of patient, unconditional love toward her. You must learn to love her with God's sacrificial love, by faith, whether you feel like it or not.[3]

Be full of joy and gladness around the house as we are commanded in 1 Thessalonians 5:16. Display your new demeanor patiently before your wife although, like any person without Christ, she tries to shake your newfound faith. We are commanded in Scripture to give thanks in all things. Thank God daily for the wife He has given you. Become involved in some of her projects. If her tastes are different from yours, let hers predominate, not only in the household decisions but in choices of vacation places and times.

Do not expect your wife to be the kind of person God wants her to be. None of us measures up to His perfect standards. So don't set impossibly high standards for her. Until she becomes a Christian, she is not motivated to be the kind of person you want her to be, let alone the kind God wants. You must accept her as she is, just as you did when you married her. Begin to assess her basic needs and make an effort to meet them.

Strive to lessen points of friction in your marriage. Be low-key about your Christian witness. Don't be completely quiet about it, however. Be sure to let her know that God's love is working to make you a better husband and father. Learn to speak the truth in love. Ask for her help. If you begin to accept your wife as she is and are patient with her, as the Lord is with us, He will put the pieces together.

Let these principles of loving acceptance and patience work for you. Through your new life in Christ you can give her a desire for a new life. Do not expect her to see what you get out of Christianity and church until your life shows it at home, where it is most needed.

You and I, in obedience to the Lord, need to make every effort to be the kind of men God exhorts us to be. Look at this Scripture verse: "Husbands, love your wives, just as Christ also loved the church and gave Himself up for her. . . . So husbands ought also to love their own wives as their own bodies. He who loves his own wife loves himself" (Ephesians 5:25-28).

"Husbands, love your wives," is a command. It is a binding directive upon Christian husbands, whether or not our wives are Christians! When we learn to love them like God wants us to, they will respond by respecting and loving us more and more.

God has laid this responsibility very heavily on us. It is no mistake that God commanded us to love (*agape*) our wives. In a sense it is a command to settle down in faithful commitment to her. This *agape* love comes from the God who *is* love and has poured out His love through the Holy Spirit into our hearts (Romans 5:5).

In contrast, wives are commanded to love (*phileo*) their husbands (Titus 2:4). *Phileo* love is human affection. I do not mean to imply that women cannot love with *agape* love, but simply that men have the greater responsibility. We are to be ministers of His perfect love. To minister means to initiate His love, and she will respond. Her response is based upon what we initiate.

Again I quote from Jerry Exel: "The command to agape his wife puts the man under another obligation also: the obligation of fidelity. The agape love of God is called 'steadfast' love in the Old Testament. It is the love that remains even if the mountains are removed and the oceans dry up. It is singleminded and faithful. In this way it contrasts with the erotic (eros) and erratic love of the average man."[4] Prove your fidelity and trust. Make her feel secure in your relationship and it will supply one of her basic psychological needs. God meant marriage to be a lasting bond, not a trial arrangement.

When we become obedient men of God, things happen as we pray and claim God's promises. Remember, God wants husbands and wives to be one. Look at your wife from God's viewpoint, and as you pray for her, claim your oneness with her in Christ. Remember, too, that if we ask anything in line with His will we can be sure He is listening and will answer and grant our request (1 John 5:14).

Implement God's principle of first loving and then being loved: "We love him, because he first loved us" (1 John 4:19, KJV). Genuinely love your wife first, and she will learn to love you in return.

Some time ago a young woman on the verge of divorce became a Christian. Her life improved so greatly that a few months later her husband went to her pastor and said, "My wife's life has changed so much! She has become such a good wife. I want to become a Christian, too." Now that you are a Christian, can your wife say this about you?

Here is a spiritual exercise. Try to recall the things that made you hard to live with before you became a Christian, and make a list of these things. Now ask yourself, "Am I still difficult to live with? If so, what makes me this way?" Let God work on your hard-to-live-with character traits.

God wants you to love your wife so much that you will not be a stumbling block to her. His love wants to win her to Jesus, but Satan wants you to be judgmental, critical and negative toward her. Learn to be forgiving and kind, and help her in these same areas. The Bible declares, "But without faith it is impossible to please Him [God]" (Hebrews 11:6). You have to see her as already belonging to the Lord. This is a divine viewpoint.

Do you have faith to win her again? Do you have the faith to persevere even if takes years before she makes a move?

9

How Much Romance?

Much is being written these days about what wives should wear to excite and inflame the imaginations of their husbands. Women seeking happiness are making books on the topic bestsellers. They are attending special seminars to develop and sharpen techniques of using all the alluring charm they can muster to captivate their husband and re-fuel the romance of marriage. This soft sell of super sex is being billed as the way to remove rocks from the marital mattress, to reopen clogged communication lines and to change the marriage fizzle to sizzle. Sex is portrayed as the "how-to" of happiness and the blueprint to blessing.

BEAUTY WHERE IT COUNTS

The apostle Peter, writing to wives, had some words about this topic: "And let not your adornment be merely external—braiding the hair, and wearing gold jewelry, and putting on dresses; but let it be in the hidden person of the heart, with the imperishable quality of a gentle and quiet spirit, which is precious in the sight of God. For in this way in former times the holy women also, who hoped in God, used to adorn themselves, being submissive to their own husbands" (1 Peter 3:3-5).

Please don't misunderstand me. There is nothing about long, straight, stringy hair or shoes with worn-out soles or pasty pale complexions that imparts holiness or attractive-ness to a woman. I want my wife to do the best she can with what God gave her. I'm sure that what outwardly passes as a special kind of sanctification does little or nothing to attract unbelievers to Christ and only succeeds in giving the wearer a smug "look what I wear and bear for the cause of God" attitude.

On the other hand, all the outward-beauty purchasables at the dress shop, the jewelry store and the beauty parlor are nothing, without love. Inner beauty is the product of God's love and will show itself outwardly in a living exam-ple that will bear much fruit.

I don't want my wife to be a sexual plaything—nor is that the role given her in Scripture. Forcing a woman into this role does nothing to build her as a person. On the contrary,

85

her self-image and self-worth suffer greatly. When a man and wife are one in Christ, their oneness is heightened in mutual, loving activity. Man's pleasure is psychologically greater when he strives to please his wife in every area rather than putting all the pressure on her to please him. His love life also becomes more meaningful when he understands her sexual needs and strives to fulfill them.

A husband who learns to please his wife in the total marriage relationship will not only build her self-image but will become more a creature of worth in his own eyes, and in hers as well. His long-range pleasure will far exceed any short-term gain.

A wife who adopts the role of a sexual plaything to manipulate her husband only helps reinforce his self-centeredness, putting him in further bondage to himself, or possibly even to her. Man, by the wisdom of our Creator, is normally the more assertive partner. He is the pursuer, and she is the pursued. Of course, this does not rule out the happy wife occasionally being the initiator of lovemaking. She will have no fear of a husband who truly loves her! Yet I do not believe it is the wife's job to lead her husband to the bedroom. I believe it is the husband's role. Nor is it a full-time occupation or necessarily a daily one.

I want to make it perfectly clear, though, that my wife always prepares for my homecoming by being neatly dressed, with her hair appropriately arranged and a dab of special perfume here and there. Probably some of the most exciting odors she arranges for me are emanating from the kitchen stove in preparation for the evening meal!

Yes, a wife can win her husband to the bedroom by imitating a bunny girl or even a burlesque queen. But she can win him to Christ only by respectful submission and by being a good example. Bedroom eyes, bubble bath and aromatic balms can do a lot for the carnal, fleshly nature, but they can never build a spiritual man who can make his wife truly happy and fulfilled.

SEX: MASTER OR SERVANT?

Those opposed to biblical life-styles and standards imagine that the Bible describes sex as something sinful or shameful. Nothing could be further from the truth. The Scriptures portray sex as a function of a body that is the temple, or dwelling place, of God's Holy Spirit. As such, sex is a holy, clean function meant to be a force so powerful as to bind two people into one in the marriage state.

One of the New Testament writers declares all things in the marriage bed to be honorable and undefiled (Hebrews 13:4, KJV). Thus he puts God's approval on proper sex within marriage for pleasure as well as for propagation.

Let us face up to the fact that God meant sex to be holy. William Temple, Archbishop of Canterbury, wrote, "It is to be recognized that sex is holy. Anyone who has once understood that will be quite as careful as any Puritan to avoid making jokes about sex; not because it is nasty, but because it is sacred. He would no more joke about sex than he would about Holy Communion—and for exactly the same reason. To joke about it is to treat with lightness something that deserves reverence."

We need to keep a proper perspective on sex. Howard Hendricks expresses this well in his book *Say It With Love:* "A good sexual relationship does not insure a good marriage, rather, a good marriage insures a meaningful sexual relationship. Intimacy, openness and honesty add depth and excitement to the one-flesh relationship as years go by."[1]

Frequently in counseling situations I find at the root of the troubled marriage a mate whose desire for self-gratification is putting inordinate pressure on the other—pressure to please, pressure to perform, pressure to initiate, pressure to be more aggressive, pressure to be more exciting and imaginative.

Sex in marriage should never be an end in itself. If you think of your wife or treat her as an object of your sex gratification, you are providing an intolerable climate for real love. If you cannot master your sex drive and passion, it will master you, and you will be embarking on a life of self-loathing.

Put God First

Living happily with your wife means letting God have first place in your life. Observe these instructions in Proverbs: "Trust in the Lord with all your heart, and do not lean on your own understanding. In all your ways acknowledge Him, and He will make your paths straight" (Proverbs 3:5-6).

Following God's instructions is the only straight path to true happiness. It begins with making Him Number One in our lives. When a man begins to reverence God and to act upon His wisdom, it brings about changes in life and behavior that result in favor with your wife and peace at home.

The goal of all psychotherapy is to bring about behavioral change. Nothing in my life has ever effected a behavioral change more than knowing Christ in a personal way. To me, the greatest evidence that God really loves us is His ability to change lives, especially broken, bruised ones like mine. Of course the evidence of His Word is important, particularly in the growth process that occurs when we apply it. It is authoritative and trustworthy. When applied, it works—as any instruction book is supposed to do. Then too, the inner effect of His Spirit witnessing with our spirits that we are His children is strong confirmation that we belong to Him. Paul expresses it as follows: "The Spirit Himself bears witness with our spirit that we are children of God" (Romans 8:16).

We are literally new creations, and how differently we feel about everything when He takes control of our lives. "When someone becomes a Christian he becomes a brand new person inside. He is not the same any more. A new life has begun! All these new things are from God who brought us back to himself through what Christ Jesus did. . . . For God took the sinless Christ and poured into him our sins. Then, in exchange, he poured God's goodness into us!" (2 Corinthians 5:17-18, 21, TLB).

All the true riches we have are contained in our minds. If our minds are bankrupt, so are we. On the other hand, we enrich our minds through getting to know God better and better. "For as you know him better, he will give you, through his great power, everything you need for living a truly good life: he even shares his own glory and his own goodness with us! And by that same mighty power he has given us all the other rich and wonderful blessings he promised; for instance, the promise to save us from the lust and rottenness all around us, and to give us his own character" (2 Peter 1:3-4, TLB).

We can only learn to live happily with the woman God has given us as we share the mind of Christ by getting to know God better through His Word.

10

Start the Day Right

Now that we have established God's priorities in marriage, we need to consider how to be successful in our sexual relationships. Becoming a Christian is not an automatic guarantee of success in all facets of marriage. Our wives may come to us in marriage partially or totally unprepared to fill their new roles—and we may not have much knowledge either.

Some time ago a young man we knew fell in love with an only daughter of a small-town businessman. These people were active in their church and prominent in their community. Their daughter, ill as a child and frail as a young adult, was romantically prepared for the marriage, but in every other way she was totally unprepared.

Her family, following her plans, staged an elaborate wedding. Yet, beyond the outward show, she had no inward preparation to face the reality of marriage. A few days after the honeymoon she called her mother to come and stay with her to "protect" her from her husband. Shortly thereafter the marriage was annulled in the courts.

Prepare or Beware

While this is an extreme case, many marriages begin with little or no thought about what happens after the wedding. Young couples spend more time preparing for the wedding ceremony than they do for the marriage. In spite of the availability of good educational material and enlightened premarital counseling, few couples take advantage of them. In addition, the level of commitment to a lifetime of marriage is low in young couples today.

Many newlyweds never surmount the difficulties encountered during their honeymoon. As a result they become frustrated wives and disillusioned husbands, unaware of the true happiness and love that can be achieved through the understanding of basic sexual principles.

Some time ago my wife and I were invited to speak to the young married couples' group of a large church. On the first evening we spoke briefly to them about happiness in marriage and set a time for counseling with them in groups as well as individually. Betty and I were much impressed with this collection of youthful lovers. Articulate, attractive, clean, they were some of the best examples of what one is looking for in young people. As we interacted with them that evening, they were crowded together on davenports and overstuffed chairs. What a happy group, we thought. There was surely no need for us here!

The next day, after a briefing session, we divided into groups, Betty with the girls and I with the men in another room. We passed out three-by-five cards and asked them to write down, anonymously, their most difficult marriage problems. Then, collecting the cards, we shared scriptural principles and counseling help for each one.

As I read what the men had written on their cards the air was electric. Their frankness was an indication of the seriousness of some of their situations. Nearly all of the hangups of this group were in their sexual relationships. Money difficulties? They probably had them. In-law problems? No doubt they had some of these, too. But, at the top of the list were problems that were ruining their sexual unions. In another room with their wives, Betty was experiencing much the same thing.

One of the most common problems listed by the men was that their wives could not achieve sexual fulfillment. Some were frank to say on their cards that they were often satisfied but frequently left their wives without this joy.

One fellow insisted his problem was that his wife never started anything. She was fine if he started the action, but he wanted to feel pursued and wanted on occasion. He wanted her to be more creative.

At the same time, Betty was getting the female variations to these complaints. One of their most frequent complaints was that men reached satisfaction too quickly, and they were left wide-eyed, unable to sleep while their husbands quickly drifted off, adding insult to injury. It never seemed to occur to the husbands that they could satisfy their spouses by other means. Some women seemed to think their husbands had abnormal sexual desires; others, that their husbands were too cold and infrequent in their advances.

A frequent theme given by the women was the indifference of their husbands toward marriage in general, leaving their wives ambivalent in their responses and hurt inwardly by the generally cool attitudes of their mates. Yet these same husbands, after retiring for the night, would suddenly become ardent lovers and expect their wives to respond similarly!

If you want your wife to become the lover you thought you were marrying, you need to study to be the lover you think you are! Women are responders, by nature. Even their physical makeup makes them a receptor for love.

Emotionally, the man usually is quickly aroused, and events of the day have little bearing on his readiness for lovemaking in the evening. Emotionally, the woman is slower in her responding role, and careful preparation is needed in order for her to respond properly.

I went into some details with these men on their individual problems, explaining their need first to prepare their wives by starting the lovemaking early in the day.

Dr. Ed Wheat, a Christian doctor whose two ninety-minute tapes entitled "Sex Problems and Sex Technique in Marriage" are most helpful, says, "The wife views the sex act as part of the total relationship with her husband. This means that every meaningful, fully enjoyable sex act really begins with a loving attentive attitude which may begin hours or even days before."[1]

START WITH "THANKS-LIVING"

Learn to discipline yourself, regardless of how you feel in the morning, to have the right attitude when you show up at the breakfast table. Remember that we are commanded to "rejoice always; pray without ceasing; in everything give thanks; for this is God's will for you in Christ Jesus" (1 Thessalonians 5:16-18) . Pray that God will make you the kind of husband you ought to be and He wants you to be.

As you shave, practice saying out loud to yourself in the mirror, "Thank You, Lord, for my dear wife and for the home she makes for me." Be prepared, then, as you enter the kitchen to say cheerily, "Good morning, darling. Did you have a good sleep?" or some other greeting. As you begin eating, resist the temptation to hide behind the morning paper (save it for later; or, better yet, keep a small radio in the bathroom, and get all the sports and financial news while showering and shaving) .

As your mind begins to go over the plans for your business or working day, share your thinking, even your fears and concerns for the day. In most cases you'll find a new ally, your sympathetic wife, with whom you have previously never shared your thoughts. Be sure to ask her, too, what her plans are for the day. Try to remember some of them, and volunteer to help her with some of her daily problems, such as getting the oil changed in her car. Call her during the day, if it is possible, and tell her you are thinking about her, and be sure to conclude by saying "I love you, honey, and I'm looking forward to being with you this evening." Arrange occasional lunches with her, if possible, at a restaurant or at home if it is convenient.

When you come home, if you follow a few more simple prescriptions, it will be a different ball game. First of all, if you are held up by traffic, business, or some other problem, call her and explain the delay. Tell her what your expected arrival time will be. She will love you for this bit of thoughtfulness and will adjust her meal preparations accordingly. She might even go ahead and feed the children and arrange a special dinner for two, complete with candlelight, love, and kisses.

Second—and this is terribly important—as you turn into your home street or driveway say, "Thank You, God, for my lovely wife and our home." Ask God for the right attitude of love and consideration as you open the door, no matter how bad you feel about losing a big order, or how close you came to being fired this particular day.

According to the Bible, what you think is what you are (Proverbs 23:7). Also the Scriptures say, "Be it done to you, according to your faith" (Matthew 9:29). If you feel the spark of romance is dead and the love affair is over, you will find it helpful to read the chapter entitled "Make Love Your Aim." And if you begin to have an attitude of praise and thankfulness, the love affair will be rekindled, and a new, more enduring romance will develop.

After dinner, be sure to compliment your wife on the meal, especially if it is something new or different. You can also learn to be a less finicky eater. Here again, it may take time, prayer, and practice to overcome your inbuilt prejudices. We all know the "meat and potato" man who is satisfied seven days a week—if that is what he gets. But mention pizza or Mexican food, and his stomach does a flipflop.

The wife and children of one of our friends liked the adventure of unusual dining, but the husband was stuck in his old routine. One day he decided to please his family. He worked up his courage for an adventure in Mexican food. Any illusions that he could overcome his finicky appetite were dispelled the instant the waitress put his plate in front of him. His face fell, along with his courage, and he began grumbling and griping so much that the family's out-to-dinner treat was ruined.

But this fellow persisted. Although he had the same problem with Chinese food, he began with simple entrees like noodles and worked up to the more sophisticated dishes. Today he is one of the first to suggest eating in a specialty restaurant—and he will order the most exotic foods.

So work at providing some adventuresome days for yourself, your wife, and the family. And when you've had a nice day and have prepared your wife throughout the day, you'll find the bedroom also a pleasant place. All this may not work the first time, but practice, practice, *practice*.

To quote Dr. Ed Wheat further: "Sexual intercourse will always be a joyful affirmation of two people's common life or a revelation of the defects, and it will either draw people together or push them apart."[2] How it works in your life is pretty much up to you, your attitudes, your teachability, and your submission to God and His Word.

This is not a how-to book on methods for sexual success. There are already enough of these on the market. This book is intended to be a positive approach from a man's viewpoint to simple principles by which you can achieve a healthy and satisfying marriage relationship and the abundant life God has planned for you.

Methodology, however, is important to a satisfying sexual relationship. If you are missing the fulfillment to which you are entitled in your marriage, if you are not experiencing the happiness and thrilling love that can be achieved through the understanding of sexual principles, then you may want to read *Sexual Happiness in Marriage,* by Herbert J. Miles, Ph.D. (Grand Rapids, Zondervan, 1967). His book is a sound discussion of the role of sex in today's marriage.

11

Communicate!

In the previous chapter, I described a counseling situation with a group of young married couples. Although many sexual problems were shared as they opened up, what many experts consider the main problem was never mentioned: *communication.*

Why should this key to a good marital relationship be so consistently overlooked? Why should communication be so important? Just what is communication? According to one psychologist, 85 percent of all conversation is so meaningless, it would be better to leave most of what we say, unsaid. Obviously, communication is not just talking.

Very simply, good communication is saying what needs to be said and hearing what needs to be heard. Just telling your wife that you are not satisfied is not telling her anything that is going to be helpful in overcoming the problem. It is important to learn to tell your wife how you feel—just as it is vital for her to learn to tell you how she feels. Verbalizing your feelings will help you to avoid some of the misunderstandings inherent in nonverbal communication, which goes on all the time. As well as learning to verbalize your feelings, learn how to hear what your mate is saying. Good listening starts with wanting to hear.

Be willing to take a look at your communication and learn from your evaluation of it. Good communication can help overcome most problems in the home.

When my wife and I were having adjustment difficulties early in our marriage, I usually reacted with silent sullenness. Perhaps not really knowing why, but experiencing vague fears and hurts, I retreated inward and secretly blamed my wife for my problems. Like most men, I blamed her for every difficulty, even in our sexual relationship. But the problem was my lack of self-control. We men have generally persuaded ourselves we are great lovers, and when problems arise, we will not take the blame any more than we will take help from our wives, or anyone else.

Elsewhere in this book, I have related how men are still brought up in the Spartan mold. Taught to conceal hurts, fears, and tears because they are shameful and supposedly

99

unmanly, we lack the ability to communicate effectively. So we withdraw into our shells. Or we cover up our anger by yelling and striking out at those we love most. Is that communicating?

Pride is a major factor, too. We may have delusions that we are great lovers, for example. Pride can also make us fearful of failure. Because I was a failure at times, I approached my wife very nervously. Occasionally my feet got cold and my palms were sweaty in my vain effort to please my wife. Sometimes I felt so threatened that I welcomed failure so I could blame her.

For years I was intemperate in my demands upon my wife. However, as I learned to love her in a new way, God's way, giving became far more important to me. I used to pray that God would temper my physical desires and give me more real love. He answered this prayer, although the answer seemed painfully slow in coming. In the meantime, God was teaching me that my wife had something valuable to say and I needed to listen to her.

Since the days when stubborn pride was the chief barrier to our communication, I have constantly been surprised by my wife's understanding and helpful attitude. Love begets love. As I tried to meet her needs with understanding and love, she tried harder to reciprocate and meet mine.

Learn to share even your sexual frustrations and anxieties with your wife. Don't defend yourself and downgrade your self-image. If your goal is to please your wife (and it should be) you both should be in a learning situation as to how this can best be accomplished. Share openly with her how she can help you. Ask her to share with you how you can best help her.

Become a good, open-minded listener. Don't interrupt or try to make points with your wife while she is trying to tell you something. If a hang-up develops in your communication and some anger and misunderstanding result, learn to accept this as an inevitable part of living together. Remember, communication is not merely what is said, but what is heard. I can never tell you what you said, only what I heard.

Learning to communicate requires practice, just as learning to do anything does. Begin listening tonight. Start with a simple routine at the dinner table. Think back over your day, and relate every happening as best you can. Be sure to ask your wife, "What happened to you today, honey?" Make this a habit, and listen, listen, listen!

In the morning ask her, "What are you going to do today, dear?" She may be surprised and suspicious at your new interest, but this will soon disappear, and she will love you more as a result of your attention and concern.

At times you will want to express to your wife just how you feel about making love to her. Restrain your eagerness; abide with her wishes if she is tired, not feeling well, or uptight from a difficult day.

Do not attack or blame your wife for real or imagined shortcomings, for you will only put her on the defensive. Openness begets openness, and if you initiate this attitude, perhaps she will feel free to share some of her fears and frustrations. Such an honest sharing will result in an intimacy that will add depth and excitement to the "one flesh" relationship as time goes by.

One psychiatrist has pointed out that good communication begins with sentences starting with *I* rather than *you*. Think this through a bit, and you will understand why. One day I mentioned this to my wife, and then she began pointing out everytime I said to her, "You did this," or "You think—" This helped a great deal, so that after a while I found myself avoiding this practice. It greatly helped our marriage.

Some time ago I was called in as a business consultant by a distributing firm. A preliminary analysis revealed that much of the poor morale of the employees was caused by the lack of good communication between the owner-manager and his work force. I discussed this with him, and he acknowledged communication as one of his weak areas.

This was a problem in his home as well. I offered some solutions for his problems in his business and ventured to suggest he could also begin practicing good communication at home. I suggested he tell his wife what happened to him during the day. His reply was surprising. "Oh, I could never do that!" he said. "How could I worry my wife about the business problems I have every day?"

Why do we have such strange attitudes about sharing our job difficulties with our wives? Under the pretext of protecting them from our worries, we deprive ourselves of the privilege of gaining their much-needed understanding and helpful sympathy. The healing balm of an understanding wife is very soothing, but she may not reach out to you unless you first learn to reach out to her. Your understanding and sharing can also help heal some of the wounds she experiences during her daily grind.

Some men, because of too tender egos or perhaps because of feelings of inferiority, will not communicate with their wives about their work-related problems. Perhaps some men think too highly of themselves and their opinions, and they cannot tolerate a differing viewpoint.

There is much truth in the old axiom "Two heads are better than one." When I first began to suspect that my wife had a head to use in our marriage relationship, I conceded that two heads *are* better than one, even if one is my wife's. With that concession, I found hers is often the best!

I no longer make snide remarks, but have learned to consult her in everything we do. This has resulted in a much closer relationship.

THREE-BY-FIVE CARDS

Another way to improve communications is to become a three-by-five-card carrier. A few years ago I was privileged to work with an outstanding Christian businessman. He was keenly analytical and sharply decisive in both business and spiritual matters. He was in great demand as a speaker because his communication in a group situation was of top caliber. He always had an abundance of fresh anecdotes and personal illustrations.

The key to his success is three-by-five cards. Whenever he hears a good story or illustration, he jots it down on one of the cards. If he is involved in something that makes a good illustration for a talk, he writes it down and shares it with his family or friends.

Someone has said, "The faintest ink is stronger than the strongest memory!" How true. Improve your ability to communicate by becoming a card carrier.

MEDICAL HELP MAY BE NEEDED

Another area needing communication is our sex life. When sexual difficulties are experienced, medical advice may be called for. Anything from poor diet to congenital difficulties may be contributing to the problem.

Far too many men begin their day with a cup or two of black coffee and a race to work without any fuel for the day. More coffee at mid-morning, coffee and a sandwich for lunch, more coffee in mid-afternoon are regular fare for many busy men. The only good meal they get is at night.

Women, much more than men, suffer from physical problems that hinder good sexual relationships. Some may stem from typical female difficulties related to conception and childbirth. Some may be with a woman since puberty and go relatively unnoticed as she learns to live with them. But with marriage, such problems may become a source of physical irritation, and a wife will unconsciously shy away from intercourse because it aggravates the condition.

There are many other hindrances to a satisfying sexual relationship. Imagine, for example, the consternation of a young bride, taught to have a bath daily, when she discovers that once-a-week bathing or showering is the habit of her new spouse. Many frigid marriages result from problems of cleanliness.

While traveling in Australia and New Zealand recently, Betty and I found ourselves facing a new dilemma—twin beds. Many of their fine motels and guest bedrooms have nothing else. There is no substitute for a good bed in the marriage relationship. The cozy togetherness following lovemaking is a must for the wife and is also very comforting to the husband.

Recently a wife who was on the Christian Women's Club speaking circuit, and much in demand elsewhere, spoke to me about her growing indifference to her homelife. Her children were grown and out of the house, and her husband seemed to have lost interest in her and was seeking his comfort elsewhere. A discreet inquiry revealed that the husband thought she was too busy with speaking engagements and evening projects to have any time for him. He complained that when she was home she was too tired to meet any of his needs. A too-busy, too-tired husband or wife will find it difficult to show love to the other partner.

I can recall several times over the years when my wife has asked me to confine more of my many projects to daylight hours so we could have some evening time together. Communication is so important!

104

You can add a little spark to your tired romance with an occasional gift. Buy her a new, frilly, feminine nightgown from time to time. Give her your favorite perfumes to wear for you. Give her chocolates if she is thin and diet candies if she is not. You can receive warm thanks for bringing flowers or plants. And have you ever considered two or three days away from home for just the two of you as a gift? I am always amazed at how much time, money and effort a man will spend to develop a single prize-winning bloom in his garden, and how little to develop a good wife.

When you see progress in winning your wife again, and you are experiencing some sexual compatibility, perhaps you could read a book together on being a fulfilled woman or a better husband. This will open new channels of communication, for when you are digesting the same truths, the nonthreatening, open atmosphere will bring greater honesty.

Don't expect your wife to give total acceptance to such books. She may have majored for many years in being critical, or she may fear she could never develop the disciplines some writers prescribe. Overcoming physical and psychological barriers to greater sexual freedom is always difficult. Circumstances can cause hindrances, too; maybe you have six children and a mother-in-law living with you, and the activity recommended is not possible.

Suppose your wife is messy and you are the neat, organized type. Just coming home and seeing days of dirty dishes piled high in the kitchen turns you off for the rest of the night. The ironing is piled high in a closet (and falls out when you open the door!), and you have to iron a shirt when you need one. Perhaps you agree with my chapter "Who Does the Dishes"—but doing the ironing is definitely out.

When I counseled one couple recently, I discovered that

105

the wife was a careless housekeeper, with a decided allergy to dishwashing. This difficulty was only symptomatic of deeper, underlying problems. When this couple began to love one another in a giving relationship, surprising changes took place in their lives. These improved their sexual compatibility as well.

MOTIVATING LOVE

The Bible tells us that man is to be continually intoxicated with the delight and ecstasy of his wife's love (Proverbs 5:19). No matter what her expertise (or what you think is a lack of it), praise her for her lovemaking ability, and she will make definite efforts to rise to the occasion. Sexual adjustment will be more rapid when you learn to incite her with God's love.

Real love, God's unconditional love, motivates. I remember one memorable walk with our youngest son when he was home on vacation. As we strolled along he exclaimed, "Dad, it's sure hard to be your son."

Surprised, I asked, "What do you mean?"

"Well," he replied, "you and Mother love me so much in spite of the messes I've been in, I'm always struggling to be a better son."

Yes, love motivates! And if you want to motivate your wife, love her in the morning, love her at noontime and love her in the evening. Praise her in the morning, at noon and at night. Let her know she satisfies you.

You will be tempted to turn into a critical, negative, complaining husband. Cultivate a noncritical attitude. The Lord Jesus admonished, "Do not judge lest you be judged yourselves. For in the way you judge, you will be judged" (Matthew 7:1-2). What a principle we have here for happy family relationships!

Put aside sarcasm, sick husband-wife jokes and reactionary defensiveness, which things only build insurmountable walls. Recently as I walked to our mailbox, a friend drove up in a logging truck. As usual, his wife was seated beside him in the cab. "Did you come for another load of logs?" I asked him.

"Yeah," he replied. "I picked one up late last night, too."

"Were you able to make it up the steep hill on the back forty?" I asked.

"Yes," he replied, "but I had to start the tractor and give the truck a push while my wife drove it."

"You have a good, helpful wife," I said impulsively.

"Oh, I suppose," he replied embarrassedly. "At least that's what she keeps telling me."

The wife looked as though she had been struck in the face by this put-down. What a miserable way we have of keeping our wives in what we consider "their place." How much better it is to praise and thank them, publicly and particularly privately. Believe me, this treatment pays off handsomely.

Perhaps your wife feels rejected. If you are not satisfying her emotional needs by your love, including fulfilling her sexually, she may feel unnecessary and unwanted. There are many subtle forms of rejection. Rejection can be a refusal to talk with her about little things of importance to her. It can be continually leaving her alone. Or it even can be leaving her alone at a restaurant while you visit some long-lost friend sitting at another table. Hunting, fishing, golf, boating, nights with the boys, even working night after night can amount to rejection. Refusing to take your wife's advice at times or failure to seek her counsel also add up to rejection. Another form of rejection is ignoring your wife's company at mealtime by hiding behind the newspaper.

A woman's response to her husband can be clouded by emotional problems. The distrust caused by a philandering

107

husband destroys a wife's sexual response. Premarital sex fuels the fire of later mistrust. It may take a long time for a man determined to heal marriage wounds to prove to his wife he is worthy of her trust. On the other hand, her yielding to a loving husband will go a long way to gain his loyalty and fidelity, and is the best insurance I know against his succumbing to the allurements of another woman.

If you have a new life in Christ it will help show your wife you are a changed or changing man, and slowly but surely God is making you into the kind of husband He wants you to be. She will forgive and even forget, for the most part, earlier transgressions of the law of love and loyalty.

One husband who came for counseling complained that his wife withheld her love to punish him. Questioning revealed he was one of those husbands that could not be depended upon to arrive home on time for dinner. When this happened she turned him off.

Whenever you are going to be late, call and explain this to your wife. Tell her the approximate time you will arrive and that you can hardly wait to be with her. She will understand, and you will begin to make promptness a priority. Be sure to share with her that you feel hurt when she punishes you like a child by withholding good things. She will abandon the system when you become the husband and man God wants you to be.

Listen to this practical discourse on sex from Paul's pen: "Let the husband fulfill his duty to his wife, and likewise also the wife to her husband. The wife does not have authority over her own body, but the husband does; and likewise also the husband does not have authority over his own body, but the wife does. Stop depriving one another, except by agreement for a time that you may devote yourselves to prayer, and come together again lest Satan tempt you because of your lack of self-control" (1 Corinthians 7:3-5).

Perhaps as a girl your wife was counseled again and again to save herself for her marriage. "Saving herself" may have meant years of emotional restraint. As a result your wedding night was a fiasco. What has been locked up for years cannot be instantly unlocked by the magic words "I do."

If such is the case, you can help your wife if you really love her. Be especially thankful for such a wife. She is a pearl of great price these days. Your love, self-control, and communication can make you her prince charming and magic deliverer. Work together in tenderness and openness on such a problem, and, if necessary, seek medical help.

One day an embittered neighbor commented to me that "marriage is a friendship gone sour." But do you really try to make a friend of your wife? Believe in her. Put your trust in her. Confide in her, and as you do, make yourself vulnerable by sharing your weaknesses. Confess your faults to her. She knows all about them anyway, but your sharing openly with her will help to make her the friend you have wanted all your life. And your best friend will become the lover you want her to be.

12

Man Under Control

The day I invited Christ into my life was so meaningful, so high and holy, that I found it difficult to speak to others about it, even my wife. Relating it now is hard, not only because it was such a beautiful experience, but also because I am afraid of giving the wrong impression to non-Christians. I am afraid I might convey to them that unless they have an identical experience at conversion, they are not really Christians. However, I must take that risk in order to tell the story properly.

God had been working in my life through the radio broadcast that Betty tuned in each morning while I was having breakfast. Then one day, on the way home from work, I invited Christ into my life. Suddenly I had a sense of His presence. At that moment I recognized what the radio minister had been speaking about when he talked about God living *in* believers. I had often pondered this and wondered how such a thing could be possible. But that day, I asked Him to come into my life, His presence was so vibrant and real that I was positive He was there.

Not only was God in my life, but at that moment the car I was driving seemed to be a special place of holiness. It actually seemed to be filled with His glory! My immediate reaction was that I was terribly unworthy to be there. I had a great desire to confess what a horribly unclean, foul-mouthed sinner I was.

As I began confessing, it seemed distinctly real that I was being cleansed and forgiven. What an experience! My sins forgiven? What a relief! It seemed as if tons of weight were lifted from my weary body and the whole world were new. At the same time, my mind was liberated from a thousand pressures. I felt like singing, so I did! As I arrived home and entered the door I found myself singing the words of a hymn, "Floods of joy o'er my soul, like the sea billows roll, since Jesus came into my heart!" These were surprising words from my lips!

A Man's Life Changed

For some time after the Spirit of God had revealed Christ to me in this startling way, I was eager to share with everybody how Christ changed my life. The change was so evident that my business partner, three years my senior and my lifelong buddy, could hardly believe it.

One day when we were traveling together on a business trip, I had my first opportunity to tell him how Christ had come into my life. He started the conversation by saying, "Pat, I've noticed the change in your life, and I'd like to become a Christian, too."

I was excited, but tried to contain my excitement as I briefly told him what had happened to me, how I prayed and asked Jesus to come into my life. We had come to a scenic spot on the Oregon side of the Columbia River, and I pulled the car over to the side of the road at Multnomah Falls as I finished the story. The capstone of the experience was his response: "Pat, I'd like to pray and ask Christ into my life, too." He prayed and invited Jesus into his life, and at that moment experienced the transformation of being a new creation in Christ.

His life began changing at a whirlwind pace. Certainly where there is the evidence of a changed life there is no argument against Christ being in control. Show me a person whose life has been radically changed, and I'll show you a person whose running from God is over. I'll show you a person who now has a proper relationship to God—and knows it!

A MAN'S LIFE HEALED

Life was very sweet and exciting as my business partner and I were able to share what God was doing in our lives each day. When Christ came into his life, he was experiencing some grave problems. God worked these out in unique ways. Later, many family members as well as others became Christians through his influence. Though he retired from business a few years ago, he has since served as the business manager of one of the city's largest churches.

Shortly after that exciting day, the operations manager of our company and I were on a business trip. As we headed north toward Seattle, I was surprised to hear almost the same words that my partner had spoken a few weeks earlier. "Pat, you seem so different, and your life has obviously changed. What's happened to you?"

As I was telling him how Christ had come into my life, I again pulled off the highway, and soon he was asking Christ to take control of his life. How thrilling! His wife was already a Christian, and their lives were richly enhanced from that moment on as they became one in Christ.

When we talk about Christ giving a new life, however, we are not talking about reformation, but transformation. Christians are literally changed by having minds remolded from within, so they prove in practice that God has a wonderful plan for their lives as they move toward the goal of true maturity. God brings this about through the work of His Holy Spirit. The new birth is the starting point of new life under God, bringing thoughts, will and emotions under His control.

Apart from understanding the ministry of the Holy Spirit in our lives, we will never have the power to be better husbands. We will never know the thrill of becoming spiritual leaders in our homes. We will miss the excitement of loving our wives into their God-ordained roles.

THREE KINDS OF PERSONS

Billy Graham once estimated that 85 to 90 percent of all Christians are living what Paul called "carnal" lives—lives of impotence, lived in the flesh, for the flesh and by the flesh. Paul wrote to the problem-riddled church in Corinth

113

about three kinds of men: the natural, or non-Christian man; the spiritual Christian; and the unspiritual (carnal) Christian.

Paul began his discourse by saying, "But a natural man does not accept the things of the Spirit of God; for they are foolishness to him, and he cannot understand them, because they are spiritually appraised" (1 Corinthians 2:14). It is this illumination by the Holy Spirit within that enables the new Christian to begin understanding the Bible. Now, for the first time in his life, it makes sense. The non-Christian, without even bothering to read the Bible, considers it contradictory and mythological. He rarely has a desire to read it.

Then Paul described the spiritual man as one who "appraises all things, yet he himself is appraised by no man. For who has known the mind of the Lord, that he should instruct Him? But we have the mind of Christ" (1 Corinthians 2:15-16).

Then Paul sorrowfully described the carnal man, the Christian who goes his own way, refusing to move toward true maturity and experience the balanced life of having Christ in control. "And I, brethren, could not speak to you as to spiritual men, but as to men of the flesh, as to babes in Christ. I gave you milk to drink, not solid food; for you were not yet able to receive it. Indeed, even now you are not able, for you are still fleshly. For since there is jealousy and strife among you, are you not fleshly, and are you not walking like mere men?" (1 Corinthians 3:1-3).

Well, there you have the three kinds of men in this world. What kind are you? Are you the spiritual Christian who has asked Christ into your life and keeps moving toward the goal of knowing more and more of the life of Christ? Are you exercising faith by obeying the Word of God as you know it better, growing and moving toward the happy,

114

well-balanced life of the committed believer? If you are the spiritual man described by Paul, with the development of the thoughts and mind of Christ gained through reading and practicing the Word of God, your life is being continually transformed into the image of God. You are seeking to bring your thoughts, behavior and feelings under the total control of God.

Or have you faltered in the Christian life, finding it impossible to live by your own human effort? Have you consigned yourself to defeat, knowing Christ is in your life, but not knowing how to let Him control it, or perhaps being unwilling to let Him control it? Perhaps you think your plan for living is better than His. Possibly you don't realize you can know His plan for your life.

Or you could be one, like so many I counsel, who lacks assurance. You can be confident that your trust in Him to save you is enough, and that you have the right to become His child when you trust or believe in Him. You can be sure on the basis of His Word and of the trustworthiness of God Himself (John 1:12). Perhaps you have asked Christ to come into your life time and time again, rather than thanking Him for coming in as He promised He would do. Do you not believe the promise He gave you when He said, "I will never leave you nor forsake you" (Hebrews 13:5)? Are you a non-Christian with Christ outside of your life? If you are, you may be frustrated, empty, and miserable, and your life out of harmony with God and man. I was this way for thirty-seven unhappy years before I asked Christ into my life.

If you are this non-Christian, you are spiritually dead. You go along with all the world's ideas on how to live a good life, but unwittingly you are obeying its unseen ruler, Satan, who wants you to follow your own evil nature with self in control.

115

You may even embrace religions of one kind or another, trying to achieve some merit with God by doing good works or gaining recognition with men. According to the true authority, the Word of God, human works and achievement will get you nowhere! The Bible says, "But God, being rich in mercy, because of His great love with which He loved us, even when we were dead in our transgressions, made us alive together with Christ (by grace you have been saved), and raised us up with Him, and seated us with Him in the heavenly places, in Christ Jesus, in order that in the ages to come he might show the surpassing riches of His grace in kindness toward us in Christ Jesus. For by grace you have been saved through faith; and that not of yourselves, it is the gift of God; not as a result of works, that no one should boast" (Ephesians 2:4-9).

A Man's Life Empowered

God has a better plan for your life. He wants you to have a love relationship with Jesus Christ, as well as with your neighbor and yourself. This relationship begins by asking Christ to come into your life. He wants you to be the spiritual man, with a life empowered by the Holy Spirit. It is so important to realize that not only does Christ want to come into your life, but He wants to be the Commander-in-Chief of it as well.

At the moment you believe, Christ moves in to indwell your body. The Scriptures tell us, "In Him dwelleth all the fulness of the Godhead bodily," then we are "complete in him" (Colossians 2:9-10, KJV). So resident within us is all the power and capability of going on and growing toward maturity.

When I received Christ into my life, I was led by the Holy Spirit to talk about Him to nearly everyone I met. In this new relationship with Christ, I was so hungry for the

116

Word of God that my wife and I began going to some night classes at a nearby Bible school. In addition, I took some day classes and went to all the Bible studies I could get to in our church. How terribly important a knowledge of God's Word is to the believer! However, there was a danger. I fell into a trap that awaits Christians everywhere: I became knowledge oriented.

A Man's Life Shared

As a new Christian, I was fruitful in winning others to Christ simply by telling them my personal testimony. Paul was a master at giving his testimony as described in Acts, chapter 22. It is recorded there how he proclaimed Christ to the mob who seized him outside the temple in Jerusalem. He also shared his personal testimony before King Agrippa; the Roman governor, Festus; and the court (Acts 26). One would think Paul, with his knowledge of the Holy Scriptures, would at least mention something about the problem texts, preach a bit about prophecy, and give his listeners some Old Testament typology. But no! Paul simply shared his testimony and left the results to God.

And so should we. When I had little knowledge of the Scriptures but eagerly told what God had done for me, I was fruitful and saw several of my friends come to Christ. But as I observed that other Christians didn't do this, I began to cease sharing Christ at every opportunity. I began to think I had to wait until I had more knowledge so I could argue, refute and convince. In other words, I began to put my trust in knowledge rather than in the Lord Jesus. Then, as opportunities came to witness for Christ, I displayed my knowledge—with some pride, too! My fruitfulness waned in the process.

I began to live a legalistic, guilt-ridden Christian life. I lost my desire to pray as well as my desire to share Christ.

Worry, discouragement, and defeat took over as I unconsciously reasserted control of my own life. I became an unspiritual man, knowing only brief periods of victory.

A Man Under Bondage

I became like the man Paul described: "For that which I am doing, I do not understand; for I am not practicing what I would like to do, but I am doing the very thing I hate. But if I do the very thing I do not wish to do, I agree with the Law, confessing that it is good. So now, no longer am I the one doing it, but sin which indwells me. For I know that nothing good dwells in me, that is, in my flesh; for the wishing is present in me, but the doing of the good is not. For the good that I wish, I do not do; but I practice the very evil that I do not wish."

Paul went on to say, —"But if I am doing the very thing I do not wish, I am no longer the one doing it, but sin which dwells in me. I find then the principle that evil is present in me, the one who wishes to do good. For I joyfully concur with the law of God in the inner man, but I see a different law in the members of my body, waging war against the law of my mind, and making me a prisoner of the law of sin which is in my members. Wretched man that I am! Who will set me free from the body of this death?" (Romans 7:20-24).

A Man Set Free

Then Paul answered his own question: "Thanks be to God through Jesus Christ our Lord! . . . There is therefore now no condemnation for those who are in Christ Jesus. For the law of the Spirit of life in Christ Jesus has set you free from the law of sin and death" (Romans 7:25—8:2).

Paul writes us in the succeeding verses that just being a Christian is not enough to keep us out of sin's grasp, and even knowledge of God's Word and commandments will not deliver us from our old natures. We can obey God's laws only if we follow the Holy Spirit and no longer obey the old, evil nature within us. When the Holy Spirit is in control, He can begin the building process, through God's Word, that will empower the new nature to override the old.

An unknown poet wrote some lines that are worth remembering.

> Two natures beat within my breast
> One is foul, the other blest.
> The one I love; the one I hate.
> The one I feed will dominate.

We let ourselves be controlled by our lower natures when we live to please ourselves. It is only in following the Holy Spirit's leading and submitting to His control that we do the things that please God and result in a life of peace and abundance (Romans 8:3-6).

Who is in control of your life? Are you living to please yourself, constantly failing and dominating your wife through "masculine power"? Or, is the Holy Spirit, who cannot fail? Or is your wife in control of your life through "feminine power," manipulating, subtly coercing and using the wiles of the gentle sex to get her own way?

Will you opt for the Holy Spirit to control your life so it is Christ-centered and able to produce the fruit of the Spirit: love, joy, peace, patience, kindness, goodness, faithfulness, gentleness and godly self-control? (Gal 5:22). It is the power of the Holy Spirit that counts!

Give up depending on your feelings and/or your knowledge. Start living by faith. "Without faith it is impossible to please Him" (Hebrews 11:6). Get rid of your guilt, discouragement, anxiety, legalism and other hangups by letting the Holy Spirit give you the overflowing life that Jesus describes in the Gospel of John: "Now on the last day, the great day of the feast, Jesus stood and cried out, saying, 'If any man is thirsty, let him come to Me and drink. He who believes in Me, as the Scripture said, "From his innermost being shall flow rivers of living water." ' But this He spoke of the Spirit, whom those who believed in Him were to receive" (John 7:37-39).

The Holy Spirit was given to glorify Christ and to empower us to live clean lives and to be witnesses for Him. So the important question facing every Christian who is not experiencing the Spirit-controlled life is, How can I be filled, that is, controlled and empowered by, the Holy Spirit?

First, you must have the desire. Like the confirmed alcoholic, you need the "want-to," or you will go along the same old path of least resistance. If you have a real, sincere desire to be a Spirit-controlled husband, thank God He has forgiven all your sins, and by faith claim the fullness of the Holy Spirit. God has promised that if we ask anything in line with His will, He hears us and grants our request! (1 John 5:14-15). He has commanded us to be Spirit-filled, Spirit-controlled, and Spirit-empowered Christians. "And do not get drunk with wine, for that is dissipation, but be filled with the Spirit" (Ephesians 5:18).

In a simple prayer, ask Him to take control of your life; then, by simple faith, believe He has, regardless of whether you feel like it or not. Believe it on the authority of God's Word and on the basis of His trustworthiness. Then, as an exercise of faith, thank Him for filling you as He said He would.

It was through coming to understand these simple, scriptural principles that I found help to become the kind of husband and father God wants me to be. It was through practicing these principles that I began to live the "up" life instead of a "down" one.

Are you a "downer"? Every day I speak to Christians who are downers. Their very hello on the phone or in person shows they are defeated. Their self-castigating words, their self-depreciating comments, their self-defeating attitudes belie faith and the Spirit's control. Instead of being positive like Paul, who would say, "I can do all things through Him who strengthens me" (Philippians 4:13), their attitudes say, "What a drag it is trying to live this Christian life. It's impossible!"

We are prone to sin. But I don't think God is as concerned with our sins as He is that we are down and fail to get up again. The successful, Spirit-controlled husband is the one who gets up whenever he gets down.

Of course, in this life we will never "arrive." But we don't need to be downers! The Bible says, "For whatsoever is not of faith is sin" (Romans 14:23, KJV). Discouragement and defeat are not of faith and therefore must be sin. So confess these negative attitudes as sin and get up from being down! Keep rebounding, keep coming back by the route of confession. If we keep on confessing our sins to Him, "He is faithful and righteous to forgive us our sins and to cleanse us from all unrighteousness" (1 John 1:9). And it is perfectly righteous for God to do this for us, because Christ died to wash away our sins.

Here are some of the wonderful results of being a Spirit-controlled husband:

1. You and your wife will begin to talk together about the Lord. What a beautiful fellowship this becomes.
2. You will develop a thankful spirit, which will help you greatly through many of life's adversities.

3. As you and your wife learn to submit to each other, Christ will be honored in many ways, bringing much reward to you both, now and hereafter.

4. Your life will begin to produce lovely fruit, and you will become the kind of person you have always wanted to be.

5. You will begin to experience unparalleled happiness together.

It is up to you. Get started! Be a man under control.

13

Two-Way Hot Line

I started this book with a prayer—one closely related to the objective stated in the introduction. My concluding prayer is that, if you are not presently living happily with the wife God has given you, you will saturate yourself with God's principles of serving, loving, and giving. Further, that you will practice using them daily so your earthly toil will be rewarded with happiness with your wife.

Prayer is the highest form of communication. We've talked about communication, but mostly in reference to dialogue with one another. Now I want to talk briefly about dialogue with God. Without talking to Him we will remain powerless, unable to learn to serve, love, or give.

Life is a continual learning experience. How unfortunate it is that many of us are closed-minded and unteachable. It is too bad that much of the Christian community sometimes turns away from all the helps offered to it. Many of us have settled into rigid patterns of thinking and have learned bad habits that we are unwilling to change. This is also true when it comes to praying. We have learned bad habits of prayer that make it a sterile, one-way monologue rather than the heavenly, two-way hot line it should be.

Talking to God

What is the reason for prayer? I believe the answer is that God wants our fellowship. He loves us and wants us to respond freely to Him. Do you love and trust Him? Tell Him so frequently.

How much can you trust a person? Only as much as you know him. How much can you trust God? The same answer applies! When you asked your wife to marry you, that was not your last communication with her. Likewise, communication with the Lord Jesus should not cease when we ask Him to be our Saviour. Cultivate a continuing communication with Him. Spend much of your prayer time in loving and praising Him, and the Lord will not withhold anything from you that you need to live an abundant and fruitful life.

If talking with God is simply speaking with Someone we love, some of us have developed strange ways of expressing our love. We don't need to approach God in an attitude of sentimental piety. We don't need to have an emotional recharging from the Sunday service or a transfusion of excitement from the weekly prayer meeting before coming into His presence. We don't need to express ourselves in King James English or wait until we learn to pray in public. We don't need to quote many verses of Scripture as we pray or assume we must wait until we are more mature Christians before we pray with others. We don't have to mimic others as we talk to God. Copying others, particularly older, more mature Christians, can lead to affectation and phoniness, and nothing in the spiritual realm is more revolting.

How refreshing it is to hear a new Christian pray. He prays briefly, to the point, with simple sincerity and sometimes humorously. Older Christians need not press on the new Christian their ways of doing things. In fact, they would do well to adopt some of his ways.

Just as good communication is essential to a husband-wife relationship, good communication is also a key to having a vital relationship with God. Christ is the head of man, and we are spoken of as His bride (Ephesians 5:32). Christ takes the male role in His relationship and communication with us. He wants us to be in perfect submission and to obey Him in every aspect of our lives as we assume the female role as His bride (John 3:29).

Christ, as our Head, is the initiator, the aggressor. He came to seek and to save the lost. As we submit to Him, He provides for perfect communication with Him. "And in the same way, the Spirit also helps our weakness; for we do not know how to pray as we should, but the Spirit Himself intercedes for us with groanings too deep for words; and He who searches the hearts knows what the mind of the Spirit is, because He intercedes for the saints according to the will of God" (Romans 8:26-27). God must feel that our communication with Him is important to have provided the way, through Christ, and the means, through the Holy Spirit.

"Men ought always to pray, and not to faint," said our Lord (Luke 18:1, KJV). He implied that if we fail to pray, we will be prone to "faint" or give up. Men, if we are going to be the leaders, the initiators, and the aggressors in our homes, our communication with God stands first in importance. One might even say that if we fail to have good communication with God, we will fail to have good communication with our wives and families.

God has given us assurance in His Word that if we ask anything that is in line with His will, He hears and grants us our request (1 John 5:14-15). Perhaps some of His answers will seem like the silent treatment as He allows us to learn what He wants to teach us from our difficult family experiences. Don't forget that even Christ, "though he were a Son, yet learned he obedience by the things which he suffered" (Hebrews 5:8, KJV).

The process of communication involves our willingness to be conformed to His image—to be like Him. When we pray, "Lord, make me the kind of husband and father You want me to be," we are actually saying to God, "Lord, make me like Your Son, the Lord Jesus!" God has to work into us, through the daily grind, the life-giving principles we need to know in order to pass them on to our wives and families. He ministers to us so we in turn can minister to them. As Finney said, "Prayer is not to change God, but to change us."

We have learned that reading God's Word is also important to our spiritual growth. When we let His Word speak to us, we can know His will for our lives. If we are obedient to it, we will develop an intimate relationship with Him. Unless we are reading, studying and obeying God's

127

Word, communication will be hindered. Prayer will degenerate into a series of memorized clichés and pious platitudes. Conversely, unless we are praying, the study of the Word will only give us knowledge, not change our lives.

If you want Jesus to reveal Himself and His power to you, the only course of action to take is obedience. "He who has My commandments and keeps them, he it is who loves Me; and he who loves Me shall be loved by My Father, and I will love him, and will disclose myself to him" (John 14:21). Jesus also promises that we can ask anything using His name and He will do it! (John 14:14). James tells us that we don't have what we want because we don't ask God for it (James 4:2). It is plain to see that the reason we don't have the power to live the right kind of lives is that we live in unbelief and disobedience.

If we are to be the kind of husbands the Lord wants us to be, we must be in constant touch with Him, the Source of our power, to do what He wants us to do. The Lord has laid a heavy burden of responsibility on the husband to love and lead his wife and family. But we will encounter only frustration and failure unless we discover the dynamics of prayer as a two-way hotline. In numerous places in Scripture our Lord has commanded us to pray. "Call to Me and I will answer you and reveal to you great and mighty things which you do not know" (Jeremiah 33:3, Berkeley). "Pray without ceasing" (1 Thessalonians 5:17, KJV). "Keep alert and pray" (Matthew 26:48).

Prayer is an attitude of the mind toward God. It is to be a continual awareness of His presence within us. I'm not against spending an hour or two a day in prayer, but if that is the only time one is in contact with God, it's not enough. Jesus made it clear we are to be in touch with Him continually.

Continual prayer is not repetitious prayer, though. Jesus

taught us in the gospels not to say rote prayers over and over again. His words were, "And when you are praying, do not use meaningless repetition as the Gentiles do, for they suppose that they will be heard for their many words" (Matthew 6:7-8). In this same passage Jesus illustrated, in what is called the "Lord's Prayer," how we ought to pray. This model prayer showed that repetition was out and plain conversation was in. Yet many of us repeat the Lord's illustrative prayer over and over again!

Putting Out the Fleece

Let us put out the fleece once and for all! We say to God, "Let's flip a coin to make a decision. If it comes up heads, God, I'll do what you say." So we flip it and it comes up heads. Then we add, "I meant two out of three times, Lord." If it is still not to our liking, we put out a "fleece," in the manner of Gideon.

Let me recount this story as it is in the Old Testament. "Then Gideon said to God, 'If Thou wilt deliver Israel through me, as Thou hast spoken, behold, I will put a fleece of wool on the threshing floor. If there is dew on the fleece only, and it is dry on all the ground, then I will know that Thou wilt deliver Israel through me, as thou hast spoken" (Judges 6:36-37).

It happened just as Gideon asked. He found the fleece soaked, and he squeezed out a bowlful of water. Typical human unbelief still lingered in Gideon's makeup. He wanted more evidence. "Then Gideon said to God, 'Do not let Thine anger burn against me that I may speak once more; please let me make a test once more with the fleece, let it now be dry only on the fleece, and let there be dew on all the ground.' And God did so that night" (Judges 6:38-39).

Gideon asked for a sign and got it. You may be asking

the Lord for signs and getting them, but it is not scriptural. Let us remember that asking for a sign is an Old Testament principle.

One day the Jewish leaders, including some Pharisees, asked Jesus for a sign. His reply was, "A wicked and disloyal generation craves evidence and no evidence shall be given it except the sign of the prophet Jonah. For as Jonah was for three days and three nights in the sea monster's gullet, so shall the Son of Man be three days and three nights in the earth's heart" (Matthew 12:39-40, Berkeley).

In other words, the only sign a New Testament believer needs is that of the resurrection. The Jews, according to Paul, considered the Good News of the Gospel foolish because they wanted a sign from heaven as proof it was true (1 Corinthians 1:22). The Bible makes it clear: "Without faith it is impossible to please Him" (Hebrews 11:6). Seeking a sign is contrary to faith. It is by faith that we are moved to pray, and it is by faith that our prayers are answered.

BARRIERS TO EFFECTIVE PRAYER

One of the most frequent hindrances to prayer is an unforgiving spirit. Jesus said, "Whenever you stand praying, forgive, if you have anything against anyone; so that your Father also who is in heaven may forgive you your transgressions" (Mark 11:25). No prayer except one of confession can be answered by God unless it comes from a heart that is free from bitterness. This is like any unconfessed sin and shuts us out from God.

The Bible says, "If I regard iniquity in my heart, the Lord will not hear me" (Psalm 66:18, KJV). Proverbs tells us, "He that covereth his sins shall not prosper: but whoso confesseth and forsaketh them shall have mercy" (28:13, KJV). In Isaiah it is written, "But your iniquities have

130

separated between you and your God, and your sins have hid his face from you, that he will not hear" (59:2, KJV). There are many other hindrances to effective prayer—for example failure to ask, or requesting the wrong things (James 4:2-3). Lack of harmony in the home resulting from treating our wives carelessly also results in ineffective prayer (1 Peter 3:7).

Peter instructs us, "Let him who means to love life and see good days refrain his tongue from evil and his lips from speaking guile. And let him turn away from evil and do good; let him seek peace and pursue it. For the eyes of the Lord are on the righteous, and His ears attend to their prayer, but the face of the Lord is against those who do evil" (1 Peter 3:10-12).

Some of us are nothing but doubting Thomases with unsettled minds turning first one way and then another. James warns us that if we do not ask with faith, we do not need to expect the Lord to give us any solid answers (James 1:6-8). Others of us have a condemning conscience and need to ask ourselves what we are doing wrong. We need to check our priorities and see if we are living for time or eternity. Self-seeking and pride are other barriers to prayer (James 4:2, 6).

PERSONAL DEVOTIONS

Personal devotions are often a troublesome area for the average Christian. We read about the devout and mature Christians who spend much time daily in devotions. When we try to imitate them we fail so miserably that discouragement sets in, and some of us become spiritual dropouts.

From the day I turned to Christ and asked Him to come into my life, I frequently prayed, "I want to be your man, God. Please make me into someone pleasing to you." Surely, I thought, to win merit and blessing from Him I

131

must follow the example of great men of God. I must spend hours having devotions and doing other spiritual things.

So the struggle set in, and with determination I tried getting up an hour earlier than my customary time. This was a hard decision to make. I was squeezing some night and morning classes at a Bible school around my business hours. In talking to some of the more dedicated students, I noted that rising an hour early for personal devotions was the thing to do.

Our professors also stressed personal devotions as the means to making us men of God. Most of them seemed to be habitually early risers for a daily time with the Lord. One pointed out that David said, "O God, thou art my God; *early* will I seek thee" (Psalm 63:1, KJV, italics added). I had to admit this seemed to indicate that David was a proponent of rising early to seek the Lord, and he may have been. However, I have since learned that "early" is better translated "earnestly," or its equivalent, as it is in more recent translations.

So my desire to be God's man led me to the discipline of getting up an extra hour early, though frankly the early-morning hours are not my best. Nonetheless, at that point in my life I was determined to be among the greats and struggled to awaken earlier. Fumbling my way into a bathrobe, I headed into the den for devotions.

I thought the man of God must read a minimum of a chapter a day and meditate therein. What a great experience this would be in my life! Surely God would bless me tremendously for this extra effort!

By the time I got to verse three in my chapter, I had forgotten verse one. By verse seven or eight, my eyelids were heavy and grating on my eyeballs. My eyes, in turn, were straining to focus on a page that seemed to swim in a liquid haze. My body seemed out of touch with my mind as I caught myself nodding into sleep. Though I stuck with this schedule for many weeks, the Lord didn't seem to help me in my discouraging struggle to be His man of the early hour of devotions.

Finally, in disgust with myself I said to the Lord, "I just can't make it this way, Lord. Please forgive me for being unable to live up to the examples of many fine brethren. I know what they do is good, but I just can't do it."

Prayer and devotions can become a work of the flesh. I was working so hard, and ineffectively, at these things that the Scriptures could well have been paraphrased as follows, "O foolish [Pat Exel], who has bewitched you, that you should not obey the truth, before whose eyes Jesus Christ has been evidently set forth, crucified among you? . . . Are you so foolish? having begun in the Spirit, are you now made perfect by the flesh? (Galatians 3:13, KJV).

I finally realized that I had begun my Christian life in the Spirit, but now, by the might of my own puny efforts in the flesh I was trying to perfect myself instead of trusting God and leaving my sanctification to Him. I was ignoring Paul's principle: "For I am confident of this very thing, that He who began a good work in you will perfect it until the day of Christ Jesus" (Philippians 1:6).

Then I began looking for a way out of devotions. I joined a Christian businessmen's organization and regularly attended their luncheons. They also had a weekly Bible study and prayer meeting at 6:30 every Wednesday morning. So I said, "Lord, I'll commit myself to this and see how I fare."

There I was, not very bright or bushy-tailed, every Wednesday morning. Some of the men seemed wide awake, and their praying was great. Others resembled me: heavy eyelids, dull mind, thick tongue, and nodding head. The main stimuli for keeping awake were the guilt feelings I endured and the threat of being asleep when it came my turn to pray. How mortified with shame I would have been if I were caught! What a relief it was when my short and ineffectual prayer was over. On Wednesday nights, I could hardly stay awake after dinner. I stuck with that routine for a year, and God blessed me in many ways in spite of the struggle to continue.

At the end of the year I became involved in some evening Bible studies, and I had to stay awake for these. So with a reasonably good excuse, I dropped out of the early Wednesday morning prayer and Bible study.

Several years elapsed, during which time I tried "a chapter a day to keep the devil away." I tried reading before I went to sleep at night. I was teaching an adult Sunday school class, and I boned up for several hours every Saturday. I also became involved in teaching home Bible studies. I frantically prepared for these whenever I could steal a few minutes. These activities seemed like good substitutes for daily devotions and helped assuage my guilty feelings— or so I reasoned.

Then what I thought to be a disaster struck. Our business, which had grown to several retail outlets, went through severe reverses. In truth, I had neglected the business and, as a poor steward, could blame no one but myself. My interests had so completely turned to the Lord's work that I had left my business in the hands of those not adequately trained or capable of handling it.

When the seriousness of the condition became known to me, I plunged back into the business, seeking to save what we had built up. Betty worked daily for two hard years with me in our struggle to pay off creditors and save the business.

During this time my spiritual life suffered deeply. My mind was absorbed with new business problems, the like of which I had never experienced. Every day while eating breakfast, I had my mind on my business problems, and I was planning the day ahead. Many times, as I was having a second cup of coffee, I would pull out my notebook or a three-by-five card from my shirt pocket and jot down plans for the day: whom I had to call, whom I was going to see, what I was going to say to the banker, and so on. This remained my routine for some time.

The Heavenly Intruder

One morning, while heading to the office, I thought again about some of these men of God who always took so much time for the Lord. My usual suppressed guilt feelings surfaced. It almost seemed that the Lord was saying to me, "Where am I in all the rush of your life? What are you going to do for Me today?"

Caught short by this intruding thought, I could only reply, "Well, Lord, You know how busy I am!" Pushing aside the unwelcome intrusion I took out a three-by-five card and headed it in my usual way, "Things to do today."

The next morning at the breakfast table God again intruded on my planning for the day. As He entered my thought processes, He seemed to say, "What are you going to do for Me, today?"

"All right, Lord," I replied. "I'll try something for You today. What do You want me to do?" At that moment the corner of my eye caught sight of a copy of *The Living New Testament* on the breakfast bar.

The Lord's answer seemed to be, "Read and see!"

I opened the New Testament to Philippians, chapter four, and read as follows:

> Dear brother Christians, I love you and long to see you, for you are my joy and my reward for my work. My beloved friends, *stay* true to the Lord.
> And now I want to plead with those two dear women,

Euodias and Syntyche. Please, please, with the Lord's help, quarrel no more—be friends again. And I ask you, my true teammate, to help these women, for they worked side by side with me in *telling the Good News to others;* and they worked with Clement, too, and the rest of my fellow workers whose names are written in the Book of Life.

Always *be full of joy in the Lord;* I say it again, *rejoice! Let everyone see that you are unselfish and considerate in all you do.* Remember that the Lord is coming soon. *Don't worry about anything;* instead, *pray about everything; tell God your needs* and *don't forget to thank him for his answers.* If you do this you will experience God's peace, which is far more wonderful than the human mind can understand. His peace will keep your thoughts and your hearts quiet and at rest as you trust in Christ Jesus (vv. 1-7, italics added).

Some time previous to this experience with the Lord, Betty and I had taken a course in writing how-to manuals. One thing characteristic about these manuals is that almost every sentence structure begins with an active verb. I made an exciting discovery that morning when the Lord spoke to me about my neglect of time with Him and His Word. The New Testament is an action book! This is especially true of the epistles. These books contain basic instructions to believers for living the Christian life. And these life-altering instructions are designed to produce character in us—the character of Jesus Christ.

In the above passage from Philippians you will see I italicized some of the sentences containing active verbs. They almost leaped off the page at me that morning. As they did, I wrote sentences beginning with active verbs on the card on which I had already written, "Things to do today."

This is what my three-by-five card looked like:

THINGS TO DO TODAY (Phil. 4:1-7)
Nov. 1, 1969

1. *Stay true* to the Lord, verse 1.
2. *Tell* the Good News to others, verse 3.
3. *Be full* of joy in the Lord, *Rejoice!*, verse 4.
4. *Let everyone see* that you are unselfish and considerate in all you do, verse 5.
5. *Don't worry* about anything; *pray* about everything; *Tell* God your needs; *thank* him for his answers, verse 6.

The concluding part of my morning reading was so great I turned the card over and wrote out verse seven.

How exciting this was! Here was God's personal instruction for me on that day, November 1, 1969. *Can I possibly do these things for the Lord today,* I wondered?

As I finished my cup of coffee and went on my way to the office, I sensed anew the presence of God. I talked with Him as I drove, pulling out of my pocket the three-by-five card and going over it again and again.

The next morning I could hardly wait to finish my breakfast and pour a second cup of coffee. I opened my Bible again to where I had left off, and God spoke to me again. Here were His instructions from Philippians chapter four for the second day:

THINGS TO DO TODAY (Phil. 4:8-13)
Nov. 2, 1969

1. *Fix* your thoughts on what is true, good and right, v. 8.
2. *Think* about things that are pure and lovely. *Dwell*

137

> on the fine, good things in others. *Think* about all
> you can praise God for and be glad about, v. 8.
> 3. *Keep putting* into practice all you learned from me
>   (Paul) , v. 9.
> 4. *Learn* to live on almost nothing—or with everything.
>   *Be content* in every situation in plenty or in want, v.
>   12.

Again the final part of my brief reading was so exciting
that I turned over the card and wrote, "I can do everything
God asks me to with the help of Christ who gives me the
strength and power" (v. 13) .

I was still excited. I seemed to get so much out of so
little reading! The day wore on. From time to time, in the
rest room, alone at lunch, during coffee breaks, I pulled out
the card and reviewed what the Lord had told me to do that
day.

Thus began my new adventure with the Lord. Often I
could see plainly where I had failed Him. My contact with
Him now seemed continuous. As I meditated on the meaningful verses on the backs of the cards, I found myself mem-
orizing some of them. My shirt pocket sometimes accumulated several cards, and I had a constant reminder that
the Lord had a priority on my time. As I read and reread
the cards, I could see He had many things for me to do
every day.

Many times since I started "coffee cup devotions" I have
reflected on the fact that their very briefness leads to writing down three, four, or five things to do for the Lord each
day. I have discovered that having a few things in the mind
beats having a dozen things in the notebook. Furthermore,
as I have come to realize the New Testament is truly an
action book, I have become a more active Christian.

How much time does it take? It takes perhaps ten or
fifteen minutes in reading and writing—the time it takes to

drink a second cup of coffee. Try it and see. The Bible will speak to you as it has to me. You no longer need to have remorseful misgivings or guilt feelings because you don't spend hours with God each day as some Christians are privileged to do.

Certainly it is commendable to spend more time in devotions, as some do, but the vital issue is not the amount of time we spend, the time of day we do it, or the amount of Scripture we read. The thing that counts is the quality of our fellowship with the Lord.

Getting Started

This method of devotions is easy to start, and getting started is the hardest part of any task. I can assure you that after getting started you will not be satisfied until you have more and more. It is even possible that your coffee-cup devotions will ultimately develop into an hour or two of time with the Lord during the morning.

Remember, "If you want to know what God wants you to do [today], ask him, and he will gladly tell you, for he is always ready to give a bountiful supply of wisdom to all who ask him; he will not resent it. But when you ask him, be sure that you really expect him to tell you, for a doubtful mind will be as unsettled as a wave of the sea that is driven and tossed by the wind; and every decision you then make will be uncertain, as you turn first this way, and then that. If you don't ask with faith, don't expect the Lord to give you any solid answer" (James 1:5-8, TLB).

My closing prayer for every man who reads this book is that he will obey the instruction given us in the Bible: "Live happily with the woman you love through the fleeting days of life, for the wife God gives you is your best reward down here for all your earthly toil" (Ecclesiastes 9:9, TLB).

Notes

INTRODUCTION

1. C. I. Scofield, ed., *The Scofield Reference Bible* (New York: Oxford, 1945), p. 1342.
2. John Powell, *Why Am I Afraid to Love?* (Niles, Ill.: Argus, 1972), p. 23.

CHAPTER 1

1. Cited in John Powell, *The Secret of Staying in Love* (Niles, Ill.: Argus, 1974), p. 18.

CHAPTER 3

1. Reull L. Howe, *The Miracle of Dialogue* (New York: Seabury, 1963), p. 106.

CHAPTER 5

1. Jerry Exel, *Sex and the Spirit* (unpublished manuscript).
2. Howard Hendricks, "The Characteristics of a Leader," cassette tape (San Bernardino, Calif.: Campus Crusade, 1971).

CHAPTER 7

1. Charles L. Allen, *God's Psychiatry* (Old Tappan, N.J.: Revell, 1953), p. 110.

CHAPTER 8

1. Jerry Exel, *Sex and the Spirit* (unpublished manuscript).
2. E. Karen Howe, "Husband, Love Your Humble Wife," *The Christian Reader*, January-February 1976, p. 32.
3. See William R. Bright, *How to Love By Faith* (San Bernardino, Calif.: 1971), pp. 11-12; 30-32.
4. Jerry Exel, *Sex and the Spirit.*

CHAPTER 9

1. Howard Hendricks, *Say It With Love* (Wheaton, Ill.: Victor, 1972), p. 82.

CHAPTER 10

1. Ed Wheat, "Sex Problems and Sex Technique in Marriage," cassette tape (Omaha: Family Concern, 1975).
2. Ibid.